# ARE YOU AFRAID?

# ARE YOU AFRAID?

Jennifer Way
and Judy Monroe

IRRATIONAL · PANIC · FEARFUL · PARALYZING · ANXIETY · PHOBIA · SUPERSTITION

**Enslow Publishing**
101 W. 23rd Street
Suite 240
New York, NY 10011
USA

enslow.com

Published in 2016 by Enslow Publishing, LLC
101 W. 23rd Street, Suite 240, New York, NY 10011

Copyright © 2016 by Judy Monroe

Enslow Publishing materials copyright © 2016 by Enslow Publishing, LLC

**Library of Congress Cataloging-in-Publication Data**

Way, Jennifer L., author.
 Are you afraid? / Jennifer Way and Judy Monroe.
    pages cm. — (Got issues?)
 Audience: Ages 12+
 Audience: Grades 7 to 8.
 Summary: "Discusses problems and difficulties facing those with phobias, including history, symptoms, treatments, and ways to help"— Provided by publisher.
 Includes bibliographical references and index.
 ISBN 978-0-7660-6977-0
 1. Phobias—Juvenile literature. 2. Anxiety disorders—Juvenile literature. I. Monroe, Judy, author. II. Title. III. Series: Got issues?
 RC535.W39 2016
 616.85'225—dc23
                          2015011771

Printed in the United States of America

**To Our Readers:** We have done our best to make sure all Web site addresses in this book were active and appropriate when we went to press. However, the author and the publisher have no control over and assume no liability for the material available on those Web sites or on any Web sites they may link to. Any comments or suggestions can be sent by e-mail to customerservice@enslow.com.

Portions of this book originally appeared in the book *Phobias: Everything You Wanted to Know but Were Afraid to Ask.*

**Disclaimer:** For many of the images in this book, the people photographed are models. The depictions do not imply actual situations or events.

# Contents

**Chapter 1** Irrational Fears ......................... 7

**Chapter 2** Disruptive Phobias...................... 17

**Chapter 3** The History of Phobias .................. 39

**Chapter 4** The Most Common Phobias ............ 47

**Chapter 5** Theories About Phobias ................. 75

**Chapter 6** Treating Phobias ....................... 85

Chapter Notes .......................... 105

Glossary................................ 113

For More Information .................. 115

Further Reading ....................... 119

Web Sites ............................. 121

Index.................................. 123

# Irrational Fears

A t first glance, Michelle seems like a typical high school senior. (Like most of the people whose stories are told in this book, Michelle's name has been changed.) She is bubbly and energetic. She's looking forward to college, and like her other classmates, she hopes to get a part-time job. A closer look reveals a young woman struggling with multiple phobias.

Michelle's phobias render her unable to sit by herself through a full day of classes. She traces her anxious feelings about school back to kindergarten. By the eighth grade, her feelings about school were so bad that her stomach would cramp up, her throat and chest would tighten, and she would often get dizzy and nauseated. These intense sick feelings, or panic attacks, eventually forced her to quit going to school.

Michelle developed other phobias, too. Eventually she found herself avoiding stores, shopping malls, and restaurants. She could not approach a drive-up window at a fast food restaurant. Waiting in line, whether in a car or on foot, was agony for her. She also feared staying home alone, visiting her friends, or sleeping over at a girlfriend's home. She never got her driver's license, she stopped going to the beach and football games, and she never went to the prom. Eventually, she stopped getting into cars or taking trips because she could no longer leave her home. Michelle's phobias had effectively imprisoned her.

Finally, Michelle got help for her phobias from a psychiatrist, a doctor who specializes in disorders of the mind. The psychiatrist prescribed Nardil, an antidepressant that helped Michelle deal with her panic attacks. A home-instruction teacher began working with Michelle in two areas: keeping up with schoolwork and dealing with her various phobias.

A big day came when Michelle first rode in her teacher's car. Three weeks later, again with her teacher, Michelle was able to sit through a traffic light change. Next, the two went to a nearby store, and Michelle bought herself a blouse. After more counseling and in the company of her teacher, Michelle sat through a few classes at school, went downtown to pick out her class ring, and to a mall.

Michelle continued to get counseling and joined a support group. She made enormous strides in handling her phobias. She eventually was able to go out with close friends, stay home alone, and go to concerts with her sister. Michelle was even able to give her mother a wonderful gift for Mother's Day—she enjoyed a meal at a restaurant with her family![1]

## Fear Versus Phobia

Most of us can name at least one or two things we fear. Joe Eltgroth sometimes became a bit anxious when he had to cross

Phobias are very real fears and can hamper a person's life. They are not always easy to overcome, but by addressing the issue and working with a professional, they can be managed.

a busy street on foot. It always took him a minute or two to look both ways several times, take some deep breaths, then hurry across the street. "It's really no big deal, though," Joe said. "I've always been able to cross a busy street, and sometimes I don't even think about it."[2]

Joe's fear is rational and reasonable. A busy street can be dangerous to cross, and it makes sense to check carefully. However, when someone, such as Michelle, becomes abnormally or irrationally afraid of objects, such as cars, or of situations, such as going to a shopping mall or going to school, then the fear is defined as a phobia.

The main element of a phobia is fear. A phobia is an irrational, abnormal, or exaggerated fear. Both fear and phobias cause psychological (mind) and physiological (body) changes.

Fear is a normal emotion. Fear and anxiety are feelings most of us experience at some time during our lives. We also may have an abnormal fear occasionally, but these fears usually are not intense enough to keep us from carrying out our everyday activities.

For example, remember the last big test you took. Even if you were well prepared, you probably still felt some anxiety when your teacher handed out the test. Maybe you could not eat that morning, you had a stomachache, or you felt jumpy and nervous. Later, just before you saw your grade, your hands may have become sweaty or your heart may have thumped a bit faster or seemed to thud louder. Those are normal reactions to a fearful situation. You had both uncomfortable emotional and physical reactions to your fear.

When someone has a phobia, on the other hand, the emotional and physical reactions are intensified. People with phobias become abnormally terrified of an object or situation even when they are in no real threat of danger. Their bodies

10

Almost everyone has had fears about failing a test or giving a speech. But there are more intense fears that can stop a person from living a regular, happy life.

react to fear in various ways, such as sweating, shaking or trembling, or quick, shallow breathing. If they see that object or if they are in that particular situation again, their bodies will react to their fear again. Many people with phobias freeze or, if possible, run away from or avoid the terrifying object or situation. This is often called the fight-or-flight reaction. If they continue to experience the phobia or if it broadens in scope, people with phobias often start to think of themselves as strange or abnormal. People often will not talk about their terrifying fears, which tends to add to their anxiety and sense of oddness.

When a phobia is so intense that it is debilitating, a person cannot function. They may stop going to school or work and socializing with friends.

Here is an example of a simple fear that grew into a phobia with far-reaching consequences. Vicki was late for a business lunch and hurried into an elevator. She nearly fell when the elevator suddenly lurched to a stop between the sixteenth and seventeenth floors. She remembered:

> *One second I was feeling only tiredness and hunger. The next second I was a raving maniac. I felt a terrible sick feeling in my stomach, my heart started to race a mile a minute, my legs felt as if they would give way. I became dizzy and faint. There was this terrible sensation of being enclosed in a solid steel box with no opening, suspended somewhere in space. I panicked, pressed the alarm button, started screaming, clawed and banged at the doors. I thought I was going to go crazy or die.[3]*

She was rescued, but unfortunately, this incident triggered her first attack of claustrophobia, the fear of enclosed spaces. Vicki could no longer ride in elevators. She quit her job because it was on the twenty-first floor. Her claustrophobia increased until she could no longer go into airplanes, telephone booths, closed stairways, windowless rooms, or subways.

## A Common Problem

Talk shows sometimes feature people who talk about how they lived for years in their homes while afraid to step one foot outside their front doors. Some talk about how they finally overcame this fear, which is called agoraphobia. These stories catch our interest, but are these people unusual or uncommon?

Anxiety disorders, such as phobias, are among the most common mental health problems in the United States.[4] You probably would not recognize someone with a phobia because most people can maintain fairly normal lives. Most people with phobias go to school or work, drive cars, go on dates, and

13

Those people who suffer from claustrophobia—one of the more common phobias—feel anxious when confined in small or crowded spaces.

marry. You may know of someone with a phobia, or you may have one yourself.

If you do, you are part of a large group of Americans. About 4 to 5 percent of Americans experience a phobia in a given year.[5] So, in a room of one hundred people, four or five have such intense, extreme fears that they qualify as phobias. Of these people, about half must organize their daily lives in some way so they can handle their phobia, as Vicki did.[6] Many people with phobias cover and hide their fears and reactions so well that the casual observer does not know about their fear.

Not all phobias require treatment. Some phobias, though, can lead to serious problems. Fear of going to the dentist—dental phobia—for example, is a common phobia. Because of this phobia, a person might suffer ongoing pain from toothaches, cavities, and gum diseases. Left untreated, this can lead to major expense as even more serious dental problems develop.[7]

The costs to people with severe phobias can run high. Some quit their jobs. Others drop out of school. Still others do not date, answer the telephone, or leave their houses. People with severe phobias have high rates of depression and alcoholism and can even feel suicidal.[8]

For those who decide to get help, treatment is usually successful and can bring a new life to those who previously suffered. Many people with mild phobias treat themselves by using self-help books or other methods, such as phobia self-help groups. People with more serious phobias may require therapy.

First, though, people with phobias need to learn about their mental health problem. Although many of them do not know much about their condition, this is changing. There is a wealth of organizations that provide education about phobias and offer treatment. The great majority of people can get control of their phobias and enjoy a full life.

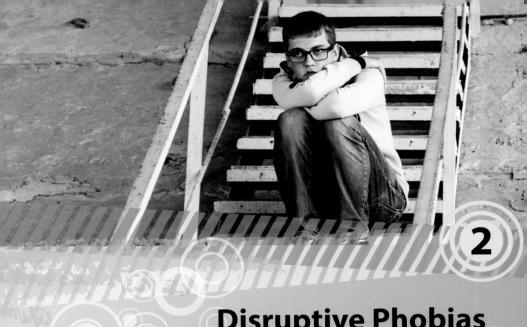

**2**

# Disruptive Phobias

There are many kinds of phobias. Some people are afraid of certain animals, such as snakes or spiders. Public speaking is another common phobia that leaves some people unable to answer questions during class. Other people have phobias that make them refuse to get onto a bus, airplane, or train. Still others have phobias that keep them away from public spaces and crowds, and they may be so overwhelmed by fear that they cannot leave their home.

Not all people with phobias suffer such intense reactions to their fears. Some lead fairly normal lives. However, some people suffer because their phobias disrupt their everyday lives. They put a lot of time and effort into avoiding their fears and try to find any possible way to avoid the object, place, or situation that seems to cause their phobias. Here are three examples of people with phobias and how they dealt with them.

*Andy started to feel anxious in high school classes when he was called on to give answers. His fears magnified in a college class where the professor randomly called on students to answer questions. To deal with his intense fear of public speaking, Andy cut classes, which led to problems in getting his college degree. Finally, he got help for his public speaking phobia from a therapist.[1]*

*Amanda Warren admitted that she avoided crowds, including parties, because of her intense fear of groups of people. After therapy, Amanda delighted her friends when she showed up for a surprise birthday party. "I know for most people this may seem like nothing, but for me, it was a celebration," she said. It was her first party in nearly twenty-six years.[2]*

*Barney experienced a different phobia. He had always loved cats, dogs, and other farm animals and decided to become a veterinarian. While he was in veterinary school, he realized that he had a problem—a reptile phobia. He remembered thinking, "If it doesn't have hair, I don't want to handle it." He stayed away from reptiles, but eventually he was assigned to work at the veterinary school's exotic animal clinic, which cared for all kinds of reptiles. Instead of running from his phobia, Barney decided to attack his own fear. He learned all he could about reptiles, so he could focus on facts and not on his terror. He also forced himself to spend time with snakes, lizards, and iguanas so he could observe and learn about them. He knew he had beaten his phobia when someone brought in a sick iguana and he was able to handle and treat it.[3]*

Andy, Amanda, and Barney all needed help to overcome their phobias. All three shared common traits when their phobias first appeared. First, they were extremely anxious in situations that were generally safe, such as speaking in a class or going to a party. Second, they avoided the source of their distress. Amanda always invented an excuse for not going to a party. Andy eliminated any chance of speaking in front of his classmates by not going to school.

Many people with phobias do not even have to come in contact with what they fear to have phobic reactions. Instead, they often worry about possible fear-producing situations. For example, Andy could feel his heart race and his palms get sweaty when he even imagined himself speaking before his classmates.

## When Fear Becomes Phobia

Fear is a normal response to a frightening situation. A pounding heart, rapid breathing, and trembling are all typical reactions to almost being hit by a car. This type of fear reaction is short-lived and is based on a real danger.

However, if people flee in great terror every time they see a spider or snake or refuse ever to ride in a car, then the fear has grown into a phobia. "A phobia is an unrealistic fear that is all out of proportion to the actual threat," explained Anne Marie Albano, Director of the Columbia University Clinic for Anxiety and Related Disorders. "The fear of spiders, for instance, would be present even when there were no spiders around. The most common fears people have are of animals or insects, natural elements like storms and water, and heights or closed-in spaces like elevators."

The American Psychiatric Association defines phobias this way, "It is an abnormally fearful response to a danger that is imagined or is irrationally exaggerated."[4] The object, such as a spider, or a situation, such as flying in an airplane, seldom does anything to the person. The person's extreme psychological and physical reaction to a spider or flying is called a phobic reaction.

Fear is a normal response to a frightening situation. For example, being dropped into a ring of hungry sharks is something nearly everyone would be afaid of.

Here is yet another definition by a therapist who specializes in treating people with phobias, "Fear becomes a phobia when it interferes with normal living and keeps you from doing things you want to do."[5]

## Three Types of Phobias

Mental health professionals divide phobias into three categories: specific phobias, social phobias, and agoraphobia. Although each causes strong, terrifying feelings, each type of phobia is different.

### What Are Specific Phobias?

Sometimes called simple phobias, specific phobias are the most common type. Someone with a specific phobia has an unreasonable, persistent fear of a specific object or situation. Typical specific phobias include closed spaces, heights, bridges, flying, insects, storms, germs, and snakes. Most specific phobias focus on animals, natural phenomena such as storms and thunder, and the human body. Mild specific phobias generally do not cause many problems, but if they become severe, they can cause major life disturbances.

The most common specific phobia is the fear of animals, especially of dogs, snakes, insects, and mice. Animal phobias often begin during childhood but usually disappear during the teen or adult years. People sometimes can pinpoint when their animal phobia began. Keith Schooler remembers that as a child he helped collect eggs on his parents' farm in Zionsville, Indiana. One day when he was about four years old, the biggest, crankiest rooster rushed toward him. Keith turned and ran away terrified of the squawking bird with the flapping wings and slashing beak. After that, Keith began to fear all birds. By the time he went to college, he had outgrown his phobia of birds. A year ago, he even roomed with someone who owned a pet canary. "I'm still not crazy about birds, but I can be in the same room with them," Keith said.[6]

Natural phenomena phobias center on natural events, such as earthquakes, floods, thunder, lightning, and storms. Dr. Stephen Garber reported that after a series of major California earthquakes, some children developed phobias. "Every aftershock sent people into panic. Many children had difficulty sleeping, feared separating from their parents for months, and remained anxious for some time."[7] To help deal with these extreme fears, the area schools established counseling programs.

Body phobias generally deal with a person's own body. Common body phobias include fear of pain (odynophobia), fear of blood (hemaphobia), and fear of cancer (carcinophobia). Unlike animal and natural phobias, reactions to body phobias sometimes include a rapid drop in blood pressure, which is sometimes followed by fainting.

**What Are Social Phobias?**

Instead of fearing specific things, people with social phobias fear situations that involve people. For some of us, falling down in public could be a little embarrassing. To a person with a social phobia, though, actually falling or thinking about falling causes intense terror.

People with social phobias have an intense fear of situations in which their activities could be watched and judged by others. They hate to look or act stupid, and because they get so anxious about their performance, they sometimes perform poorly in public. Their real or imagined bad performance then intensifies their worries. Some people with social phobias feel such stress about possibly embarrassing situations that they spend a lot of time and energy avoiding any public activities.

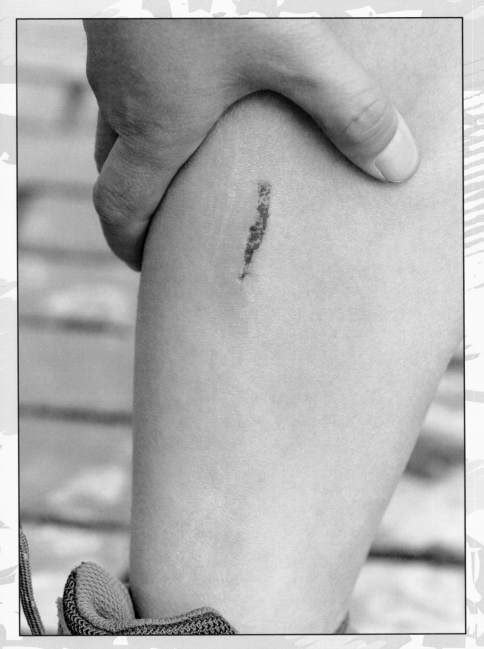

Hemaphobia is a fear of blood. Although no one likes bleeding, being genuinely afraid of blood is irrational, therefore it is considered a phobia.

Others will go ahead with the activities, but will suffer terrible anxiety before, during, and after the event.

Shyness and social phobias are not the same. Shy people often feel self-conscious. They may feel uncomfortable meeting or talking with strangers but can force themselves to do so if necessary. People with social phobias are more than shy. They avoid any situation with people they feel are scary or threatening and become anxious before and during any public event.

The most common social phobia, according to the American Psychiatric Association, is speaking in public. The list of other potentially threatening activities for people with social phobias includes just about any activity near or involving people—dating, eating or drinking in a restaurant, using a public restroom, casual conversations especially with strangers, blushing, going to a party or nightclub, dancing, buttoning a coat, signing a personal check or credit card slip, coughing during a concert or play, choking on popcorn during a movie, falling while ice skating, or playing a game of basketball.

Some people with social phobias worry that their hands or head will shake as they eat, write, or perform other daily activities. This leads them to avoid banks, restaurants, and other public places. They often cannot maintain much eye contact when talking with others and will cross the street to avoid talking with an approaching friend or acquaintance. Parties rate high on their list of things to avoid, and they prefer to do things alone and away from the eyes of others.

People with social phobias generally avoid playing sports, especially competitive games. Sometimes athletes form a phobia as a reaction to the constant pressure to perform well. For example, a professional football player who was formerly an excellent athlete could no longer kick well during a live game, when tens of thousands of cheering fans watched. His kicks became short, wobbly, and off the mark. During practice with no fans around, his kicks were great—long and accurate. Therapy helped him overcome his social phobia and return to his position.[8]

John is another person with a social phobia. His phobia affects every part of his life. As a child, John was rather shy and quiet, but he laughed and played games with his friends. By his early teens, John began withdrawing from his friends. He went to fewer and fewer parties and concerts and preferred to study or to listen to music alone in his room. Always an excellent student, John was accepted into a top-ranked college. He packed his suitcases, said good-bye to his parents, and left home to live in a dorm. He did not make a single friend and stopped going out of his room except for quickly eaten meals. Finally, unable to cope with any part of college life, John dropped out before the end of the first semester and returned to live at his parents' home. He feels safest when he is alone in his room listening to music.

John described what it was like for him in college:

> *Every time I walked into a classroom, I would start sweating profusely, my mouth felt like it was full of cotton, and I didn't think I would be able to talk—even if my life depended on it. Then I would start to feel this intense heat rise up through my arms and legs and face, and I would turn bright red—as if my entire body was blushing.[9]*

John's type of social phobia is so severe that it interferes with his daily life, school, and almost all of his relationships outside of his immediate family. This degree of social phobia is so emotionally painful that many who suffer from the disorder avoid all social contact.[10]

### What Is Agoraphobia?

People with agoraphobia often experience one of three terrifying fears—fear of being alone, fear of leaving home, or fear of being caught someplace where it is hard or awkward to leave. They are afraid of being in public places if they think escape is impossible or difficult.

Someone with agoraphobia may seem to have the same symptoms as someone with a social phobia. Both, for example, may not go to parties, but their reasons for not going differ. People with social phobias fear people looking at them and judging their clothes or their hair, or they cannot talk to strangers. People with agoraphobia avoid parties because they have an intense fear of a panic attack occurring at the party.

Panic attacks are unexpected and unexplained periods when someone reacts to an extreme fear; however, nothing specific has caused that fear. Panic attacks seem to have no cause and hit suddenly with no warning. Although they usually last for only a few minutes, they can cause intense, frightening feelings and body changes. Not all people will have all these symptoms, but at least four of the following symptoms will usually appear during a panic attack: a racing heart, shortness of breath, chest pains, sweating, heart pounding, fainting, dizziness, hot or cold flashes, trembling or shaking, nausea, tingling, and weakness. For many, a terrible fear takes over during the panic attack— that they will go crazy, completely lose control, or die. About one third of those who suffer from panic attacks will eventually develop agoraphobia.

People with agoraphobia display a wide range of intense fears. Some stop using public transportation or going to shopping malls or supermarkets because they fear being trapped in a public place. Others shy away from wide open spaces and will not drive down wide streets or walk in a large open field. Long hallways in buildings scare some people with agoraphobia. Some cannot leave their own homes to go anyplace unless they are with a trusted friend or relative. Some can only travel on a fixed route, such as from home to work or school then back home. Other people with agoraphobia have not stepped outside their homes in months or years. Until she went to a therapist for treatment, one woman with severe agoraphobia had not gone beyond the boundaries of her house and yard in forty years.

People with agoraphobia tend to avoid situations or places that they think may bring on a panic attack. They also fear that

Those with agoraphobia are generally afraid of not being able to escape a place or situation. Staying at home is comforting.

they will not be able to quickly get to a place where they feel safe or to a person with whom they feel comfortable. For some people with agoraphobia, only a handful of places are terrifying, but for others, nearly every place holds a threat of danger.

## Who Develops Phobias?

Phobias are more likely to develop in women than in men. The American Psychiatric Institute for Research and Education (APIRE) reports that about 7.8 percent of Americans have phobias. The researchers also found that phobias were the most common mental health problem among women of all ages and the second most common mental health problem among men older than twenty-five.[11]

Specific phobias, especially animal phobias, are common in children. However, anyone can develop a specific phobia at any age. Women are twice as likely as men to develop a specific phobia.[12]

Social phobias generally take hold more slowly than do specific phobias or agoraphobia. Social phobias often start when people are between the ages of fifteen and twenty, and they affect slightly more females than males. People may suffer from only one social phobia, or they may have several at one time.[13]

People with social phobias generally have limited school, work, and social lives because they interact poorly with other people. If they are untreated, they can develop agoraphobia, alcoholism, or depression. Some people with social phobias may become suicidal.

Agoraphobia is the most disabling phobia.[14] It usually starts when the person is between the ages of eighteen and thirty-five, and it affects nearly three times more women than men. It can start suddenly or slowly. There is no single type of person who develops agoraphobia.

Phobias can occur in anyone at any time. They can develop slowly or appear suddenly. Women are more likely than men to develop most phobias.

## Superstitions and Hypochondria

Phobias are not related to superstitions or hypochondria. A superstition is an irrational belief that an object, action, or circumstance will influence the outcome of an unrelated event. Superstitions are widely known and often traditional beliefs that are shared by many people. People generally do not have panic attacks because of their superstitions. Usually, people suffer no lasting or harmful effects from their superstitions. If someone avoids black cats on Halloween, for example, this superstition lasts a short time—about twenty-four hours. A phobia lasts much longer than a day.

People who have hypochondria have persistent thoughts that they are ill or likely to become ill. They suffer real pain, although a physical illness is neither present nor likely. They often go to the doctor frequently. Hypochondria often begins when a person is a teenager, but it tends to get worse in their thirties and forties. The symptoms of hypochondria remain vague and chronic and often move to different body parts.

Someone with an illness phobia reacts differently than a hypochondriac. A person with an illness phobia has an unreasonable fear of a specific illness, such as cancer or AIDS. This person's extreme fear is sometimes triggered when a close friend or relative develops the illness.

## Phobic Reactions

Carol Schatz had a driving phobia that started when she was in her late twenties. She described it this way:

> *You're at the wheel, and your stomach is slightly queasy. A soft but steady ringing starts in your ears. You try to get a grip—in this case, on the wheel. You tell yourself it's fine, you know how to drive, you've never crashed. . . . When you force yourself to start driving, your head feels like it's filling with helium and is*

Some people have a fear or driving. This phobia manifests itself in physical symptoms when the person gets behind the wheel.

*desperately trying to detach itself from your body. Your heart is making far too much noise.*[15]

Fred, a person with social phobia, was required to take Spanish in the seventh grade. This was a terrible experience for him because he had to speak the language in front of his classmates and teacher. He remembered:

*I performed very poorly and was always embarrassed. I could barely get the words out and knew all the other students noticed my problem. My heart would beat fast, my hands would sweat, and my mind would become dizzy. Every morning I woke up with a stomachache and a general frightened, anxious feeling.*[16]

31

Most of us get nervous speaking in front of a group. We are all familiar with the racing heartbeat and sweaty palms associated with public speaking.

Many people with phobias feel a little anxious most of the time. They worry a lot, even when they are not aware of doing so. Not all people with phobias experience the same symptoms when they become afraid, and their symptoms can vary during each phobic reaction.

When their fear is triggered, a person with a phobia might feel dizzy or anxious, and they might shake, faint, tremble, or sweat. Their stomach may churn, and they may feel nauseated, hot, or numb. Some have trouble standing because of wobbly knees. They can have breathing difficulties or feel confused or out of control. Most will feel strong and irrational panic, dread, horror, or terror and will want to—or actually do—run from the fearful object or situation. These overwhelming symptoms may cause some people with phobias to fear that they are dying, having a heart attack, or going crazy.

After their intense fear reaction, many people with phobias feel tired and shaky. If this is a first attack, they may feel alarmed. For longtime sufferers, an attack often brings anger or embarrassment because they could not prevent or stop the attack.

## Other Problems Related to Phobias

The physical and emotional pain caused by severe phobias causes a lot of suffering. Other problems tend to multiply as a result of the phobia. Some people with phobias resort to drinking or taking drugs to help them cope. Researchers report that about 20 percent of people with social phobia and agoraphobia develop alcoholism, and about half of those suffer from depression.[17]

Phobias may cause some people to lose self-esteem. Many silently scold themselves for not being strong enough to overcome their fears. Because they can no longer work, some people with severe phobias slide into poverty. Family members, friends, and coworkers may not understand or believe how bad the person feels. Relationships and friendships sometimes dissolve, and families can fall apart.

One young woman still feels sad because she could not leave her home to take her baby son to a nearby park or for rides in his stroller. "The thought of opening the front door was enough to give me the shakes," she said. "I let agoraphobia steal the joy from my life for nine years."[18]

## Famous People With Phobias

Some famous people have suffered from phobias, including:

*Carly Simon*, singer and songwriter, could not perform live for eight years because of topophobia, or severe stage fright.[19]

*Willard Scott* suffered from social phobia before he became a well-known television weather forecaster. He has explained being shy and having a social phobia this way: "I compare it to cutting your fingers as opposed to having a train run over you. The difference is that dramatic."[20]

*Harry Houdini*, the world-famous escape artist, had claustrophobia. He could cope well when locked into tight spaces during his escape acts. However, when he accidentally was trapped in tight spaces, he had phobic reactions.[21]

*Aretha Franklin*, singer, has aerophobia.[22]

*Frederick the Great*, eighteenth-century King of Prussia, could not wash himself because he was terrified of water (aquaphobia). His servants cleaned him with dry towels.[23]

*Napoleon Bonaparte*, Emperor of France, was terrified of cats (ailurophobia).[24]

*Edgar Allan Poe*, author, feared closed spaces. He drew on his own claustrophobic reactions when he wrote some of his great short stories, such as the "The Black Cat" and "The Premature Burial."[25]

**Sigmund Freud** became world famous for his development of psychoanalysis, a form of therapy. He often wrote about his own agoraphobia. He also feared death, traveling by train, and crossing wide streets.[26]

**Howard Hughes** was probably the most famous and wealthy person with multiple phobias. First, he developed a fear of germs (mysophobia) and always wore gloves before touching anyone. He went through four boxes of tissue paper every day because he wiped off everything he touched or received. As he grew older, he developed agoraphobia. Finally, he developed panphobia—a fear of everything and everyone. For example, Howard Hughes "saw a 189-foot-high one-million-dollar sign in front of the hotel across the street. He was immediately convinced it was going to fall on his penthouse. When the owners refused to take down the sign, Hughes bought the hotel."[27]

**Howie Mandel**, actor, comedian, and television host, has mysophobia and will not shake hands with anyone without wearing latex gloves.

# Famous People With Phobias

**Carly Simon**

**Howie Mandel**

**Harry Houdini**

**Aretha Franklin**

# Famous People With Phobias

**Napoleon Bonaparte**

**Edgar Allan Poe**

**Sigmund Freud**

**Howard Hughes**

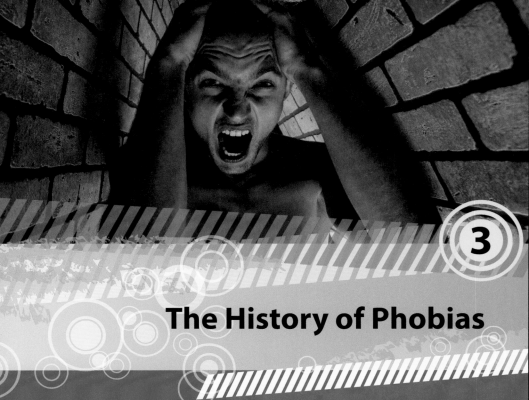

**3**

# The History of Phobias

$P$*hobia* is a word coined from the Greek word *phobos*, which means "fear, terror, and panic." Phobos was also the name of a god in Greek mythology who struck fear and panic into his enemies during war. Greek warriors tried to use the power of this fear by carrying battle shields with the god's face etched on them.

Although the word *phobia* was not used until the late eighteenth century, fear sicknesses and similarly named conditions have been written about since ancient times. While phobias and phobic reactions have been written about throughout recorded history, it was not until the twentieth century that a scientific understanding was developed.

## The Earliest Writing About Phobias

The Greek physician Hippocrates lived from about 460 to about 377 B.C.E. and is known as the father of medicine. He recorded detailed descriptions of people with phobias. He wrote of a man named Damocles who could not go near an overhang, over a bridge, or even near a shallow body of water. Another man, Nicaros, could happily listen to flute music during the day. However, at night hearing a flute caused him to feel extreme fear. Hippocrates described how Nicaros reacted, "As soon as he heard the first note of the flute at a banquet, he would be beset by terror and said he could scarcely contain himself."[1]

In 1621, English clergyman Robert Burton wrote *Anatomy of Melancholy*, in which he described people with various intense fears. Some could not leave their homes for fear that they would faint, become sick, or die. Another could not cross a bridge, go near water, or go near steep hills. He also described a person who was afraid of being locked in rooms and who could not go into crowds or public places. During Burton's lifetime (1577–1640), fearful and unusual behavior such as this was often thought to be caused by witchcraft, demons, or evil spirits.[2]

John Bunyan (1628–1688), English author of *The Pilgrim's Progress*, described his own increasing fear of ringing bells and church steeples. At first, he worried that the bell would fall straight on him. Then he feared that the bell would bounce off the wall and kill him. His fear continued to grow until he actually thought the steeple would come crashing down, fall on his head, and kill him.[3]

A. Le Camus (1722–1772), a French surgeon, wrote the first comprehensive medical study on phobias in 1769. He named his book *Des Aversions*, which translates to *On Aversions*.

Father of medicine Hippocrates was among the first to record observations related to phobias in humans. Throughout history, people have been crippled by irrational fears.

Samuel Johnson (1709–1784), an English author, noted his own fear of crowded places. He asked to be excused from jury duty because he would nearly faint in crowded places.

Benjamin Rush (1745–1813), a noted American doctor, wrote an article in 1789 that gave his definition of phobias, "I shall define phobia to be a fear of an imaginary evil or an undue fear of a real one."[4] His definition is still used today. He also named eighteen specific phobias, including fear of dirt and fear of rats.

## Growing Knowledge

During the nineteenth century, people began to study how the mind works. Phobias were increasingly described in psychiatric studies and writings. Psychiatry is the branch of medicine that deals with the diagnosis, treatment, and prevention of mental and emotional disorders.

The first definition of agoraphobia was published in 1872 by the German psychiatrist Otto Westphal (1833–1890) in his book *Die Agoraphobie*. Westphal decided to use the word agoraphobia to describe this fear. His patients all had a terrible phobia of streets or public places. Agora is the Greek word for market.

In *Die Agoraphobie*, Westphal described three people with agoraphobia. Each person dreaded and avoided walking through certain streets or areas in town, especially when the streets were deserted and all the stores were closed. All felt more comfortable walking in these areas if trusted people came with them. He also noted that the thought of going to these places was as terrifying to these people as actually going. He wrote that one of the people with agoraphobia drank alcohol to give him courage to deal with his fears. Westphal's book drew the attention of researchers and doctors in France, England, and Germany.

For several decades, people wrote about and named many other phobias. Many of those names are still used today. In Austria, Sigmund Freud (1856–1939) contributed great work on understanding phobias. He was one of the first people to describe the feelings of anxiety that occur with phobic reactions.

Throughout the twentieth century, researchers and therapists in the United States developed better definitions of phobias for the Diagnostic and Statistical Manual of Mental Disorders (DSM). This book helps doctors, psychiatrists, psychologists, and other health professionals diagnose phobias and other mental disorders and illnesses. The DSM was first published in 1952 and listed all the types of mental disorders known at that time. It was revised in 1968, 1980, 1987, 1994, 2000, and 2013.[5]

By the late 1970s, research on the brain and brain chemistry helped scientists better understand human behavior and emotions. Along with research on mental health, this research led to increased knowledge about phobias.

In the early 1980s, researchers gathered information on the number of Americans suffering from phobias. At that time, the National Institutes of Mental Health (NIMH) conducted the first survey of mental health in the United States, the Epidemiological Catchment Area (ECA) survey. Researchers interviewed nearly twenty thousand people in five cities: Baltimore, Maryland; New Haven, Connecticut; St. Louis, Missouri; Durham, North Carolina; and Los Angeles, California. This survey uncovered a startling fact—anxiety disorders, including all phobias, are the most common mental health problem in the United States.

Engraved from the Original Picture in the possession of D.D. Hosack. Painted by Sully 1812. Leney sc.

BENJAMIN RUSH M.D. L.L.D.

Eighteenth-century medical doctor Benjamin Rush's definition of phobias is still in use today. Rush recognized phobias as irrational fears of real things or fears of imaginary things.

The results of the first National Comorbidity Survey (NCS) in 1992 agreed with the results of the ECA survey. Follow-up studies were completed in 2002 and 2004. Since these studies were published, people have heard and seen a lot of information about phobias in newspaper and magazine articles, on television, in books, and on the Internet. The NIMH spends millions of dollars each year on the causes and treatments of phobias and other anxiety disorders. This information has reached many people with phobias, and it has helped them understand their phobias and the various treatments available.

# 4

# The Most Common Phobias

Hundreds of phobias have been named, but researchers have found that about one hundred phobias account for the phobias most people suffer from. Many of the names given to phobias come from Latin words. For example, bee in Latin is api, so a fear of bees is called apiphobia.

People can develop phobias about nearly anything. Since ancient times, people all over the world have had phobias about various things, places, and situations. People living today can develop phobias about things that did not exist hundreds of years ago. For example, a fear of flying is a common phobia today, but airplanes did not exist until the Wright brothers' flying machines launched a whole new industry.

All people with phobias share one important thing in common—intense fear. Fortunately, many people are able to

47

overcome their phobias either on their own or through some type of help and support.

## An A–Z List of Common Phobias

**Acrophobia**—A fear of heights is one of the most common phobias in the United States. More than eight million people suffer from this fear, but few seek treatment. People with acrophobia might fear being on the top floors of buildings or at the top of a hill or mountain. Many get nervous if they are near or on bridges, rooftops, and overlooks. People often develop this phobia because they are afraid of falling from a tall place and hurting themselves. Sometimes they may actually want to jump off a tall place to get away from it.

*Mildred has never gone inside a skyscraper, but Mildred fears just standing on a chair. When she was a student librarian, she broke into a sweat every time she had to climb a ladder to reach a high shelf. She has arranged her lifestyle around her severe phobia, which has followed her since she was a child. Mildred's home has one floor and no basement. She chose to be a children's librarian because that collection of books is usually on the first floor or in the basement of a library. She will not go to a party if she has to climb stairs or use an elevator. She has not seen a live sports event in years because she cannot sit in the bleachers. Crossing bridges is also out of the question for Mildred because she has gephyrophobia—a fear of crossing bridges—too.*

People with acrophobia, such as Mildred, sometimes suffer from gephyrophobia, as well, because both phobias cause a person to imagine being "drawn over the edge and not be able to resist the impulse to plunge or fall from the height."[1]

**Aerophobia**—One of the most common phobias in the world is fear of flying. This can add up to a lot of problems, especially for people who need to travel by air because of their jobs. Many people with aerophobia will not even go near an airplane. They list many reasons to be concerned—they could get sick on a rough flight, the airplane could crash, no one would control the airplane if the pilot got ill, or they could die. They worry that they will lose control in the airplane and embarrass themselves or go crazy. Others fear death or being separated from loved ones. Some fear being trapped and unable to leave the airplane, being rejected by others on the flight, and giving up control to the air crew. These reasons reflect specific fears, use to such as fear of being alone, fear of being rejected by others, and fear of being trapped and hurt.

Treatment for aerophobia works well, especially when people get accurate information about airplanes and flying. Some local airports sponsor courses for people who are afraid to fly. One treatment program is SOAR, which offers DVDs that people with aerophobia can watch and use to learn coping techniques.

*Hillary decided to try a similar treatment program when her fear of flying developed into a phobia. As a kid, Hillary loved to go on airplanes. "I loved the smell of jet fuel, the peanuts, the playing cards, the free cans of Coke," she remembers. Somehow, she started to fear flying. One day when she was about twenty, she was on a rocky flight and became panic-stricken and afraid she would die during the flight. After that, she developed all kinds of rituals to help her through a flight, such as carrying good-luck charms or sitting only in certain spots on the airplane. Her flying companions got tired of sympathizing with her fears. Finally, four years later, she*

Aerophobia is a fear of flying. This phobia can be treated with information about the flight process and the aircraft. Relaxation techniques can also help.

*realized that she had a phobia and enrolled in a workshop called Freedom From Fear.*

*The goal for her group of twelve people was to fly from New York to Boston and back by the third day of the workshop. First the group learned technical information about flying. Then they practiced ways to cope with their fears, such as deep breathing and relaxing. Next, all twelve got on the plane and explored the controls, opened the doors and windows, and walked around to help make them more comfortable on the airplane. Finally, everyone took the trip and did fine. After taking other flights since then, Hillary says she is not crazy about flying but still likes the peanuts.*[2]

**Agoraphobia**—This fear has been recognized since ancient times as fear of the marketlace. People with agoraphobia fear leaving familiar homes or places. They dislike going into streets, unknown buildings, city buses or cars, or crowded places because they fear panic attacks. To increase their comfort level, some people with agoraphobia prefer to go to new places with people they trust and know well in case they panic. Current studies have found that about twice as many women as men experience agoraphobia. According to Dr. Ronald Doctor, "Agoraphobia is the most common phobic disorder for which people seek treatment. It is also the most disabling."[3]

**Ailurophobia**—For most people, soft, furry cats make great pets. People with ailurophobia would disagree, however. They say that cats can scratch or hurt them or that they dislike a cat's large eyes staring at them. People with cat phobias generally avoid cats, but if they see a picture or photo of a cat or see or touch a live cat, they panic. They may have a hard time breathing, and their heart may race. These phobic reactions may appear to be the same as an allergic reaction to a cat, but they are not. An allergy is when the body physically reacts badly to a specific substance. Allergic reactions include trouble breathing, rashes, sneezing, itchy and watery eyes, and stomach problems.

**Amaxophobia, ochophobia**—Sometimes people are afraid of driving or riding in vehicles, usually because of claustrophobia.

*Jerry's fear of taxis threatened his income because he was a taxi driver. He started out driving in New York City, but he became increasingly terrified when he had to drive through the city's tunnels. He admitted to having claustrophobia, and he knew the reason for this. As a child, he was locked in a dark closet when he misbehaved. His fear spread to enclosed phone booths and elevators and then to tunnels.*

*Jerry moved to another city and hoped to leave his fears behind. Instead, he now could not go to the movies or to church unless he sat in the aisle seat, and he did not go to other public places unless he felt he could easily escape. He continued to avoid elevators, but now he feared stairs. He then realized that he could no longer drive his taxi in heavy traffic. When his fear grew so that he could not sit behind the wheel of his cab, he sought treatment because "that job was the only thing I knew how to do."[4]*

**Apiphobia**—The fear of bees often starts with a general fear of flying insects. Children start fearing flying insects from watching others react or by seeing scary movies about bees or flying insects. People who are afraid of bees report that the tiny yellow-and-black insects are attacking them. If people have an extreme fear of bees, they drive with the car windows always tightly rolled up or they stay indoors during the day. As with ailurophobia, people who are allergic to bee stings differ from

It may be hard to believe, but some people are afraid of the common house cat. People who suffer from ailurophobia react not only to seeing a cat in person, but even to pictures of cats.

53

people with apiphobia. In fact, bee stings can be fatal to some people who are allergic.

**Aquaphobia**—This phobia was described as early as the first century A.D. People with this phobia are afraid of water. Some people fear swimming, bathing, or seeing or imagining running water or bodies of water, such as lakes, streams, or rivers. Sometimes people cannot go into water over their heads, although they know how to swim. Others avoid being on the water's surface and stay away from boats, canoes, or ships. Carol Murray refuses to take showers and only bathes in a bathtub. She explained, "I feel panicky in a shower. I don't like the water hitting my face and running down my body. My heart starts to race, and my breathing gets short and choppy. I'll go into a pool, but only if the water is lower than my waist."[5]

The fear for people with aquaphobia often began when they were babies or small children. They may have nearly drowned in a pool or in a larger body of water. Parents or grandparents may have taught the child the fear by demonstrating it themselves or by forcing the child into deep water before he or she could swim.

**Arachnophobia**—At one time, spiders played a role in medicine. To cure fevers, doctors in the mid-eighteenth century recommended eating spiders spread on top of bread and butter.[6] Today, the fear of spiders affects more women than men. People with strong arachnophobia try to avoid spiders by fumigating their homes regularly, or treating their homes with fumes to kill pests. They carefully wash all fruits and vegetables, and they check all bags and boxes for any hidden spiders. For some people, this fear may be based on a widely held myth. Many people believe that spiders are poisonous, but few species of deadly spiders actually live in the United States.[7]

Aquaphobia is a common fear of the water. Some aquaphobics fear swimming pools, lakes, or oceans, while others fear the shower. These people feel like they will drown.

**Astraphobia**—People who fear lightning often will not go outside during storms or if lightning is predicted. They check weather reports often. If lightning occurs, they may hide in small, tight places, such as closets, or they may hide under beds. Some people develop this fear from observing the reactions of parents or grandparents who are afraid of lightning. Other people may have a bad experience with lightning during a storm.

**Batrachophobia**—If you fear snakes and frogs, you have bactrachophobia, a fear of reptiles. Some people react to pictures, descriptions, or the sight of these animals; they fear their webbed feet, long hind legs, and skin. Others simply fear actually touching these creatures.

**Botanophobia**—Have you ever heard that people who are ill should not have flowers left in their rooms at night? People with botanophobia believe this myth. This idea may have developed in ancient times from fairy tales told to children about plants and flowers that were hiding places for evil spirits. During the night, the evil spirits would sneak out and hurt the sick person. Some people with botanophobia say that plants use up oxygen needed by people. Some people with pollen and other plant allergies develop botanophobia because they fear the rashes, sneezing, and other symptoms caused by their plant allergies.

**Brontophobia**—Although there are people who find thunderstorms exciting, people with brontophobia avoid thunder whenever possible. They may repeatedly check the weather forecast online to determine if and when thunder is approaching. If it is predicted, they often stay home. During episodes of thunder, some people with brontophobia hide in small spaces, as people with astraphobia do.

**Claustrophobia**—Many people dislike feeling trapped. However, people with claustrophobia actually panic when they are in a closed place. Many report that they cannot breathe; they feel as though they are suffocating. People with claustrophobia react to all types of places—closets, subways, tunnels, telephone booths, caves, elevators, small rooms, crowds, cars, buses, airplanes, and many types of buildings. Some people with claustrophobia can manage a few specific enclosed spaces—cars or buses but not trains, for example. Crowds, or even the thought of crowds, bring terror to people with claustrophobia. They avoid crowds and severely limit their activities. Sometimes people with claustrophobia can handle being in an enclosed place as long as a door is left open. Others may panic if they are in a room with a shut window or if the shade, blind, or curtain covers the window.

Sometimes claustrophobia results from a frightening dream of being trapped in a closed space. When the person awakens, the dream may be forgotten, but the feelings of fear remain. For others, a real-life experience may trigger claustrophobia.

*Bonnie remembers that as a young girl, she could not find her mother at home. She went to a neighbor's house to look for her mother. Not hearing anyone, she began walking through the neighbor's house. When she climbed into the attic, the door, perhaps caught by the wind, slammed shut. She could not open it, and she sat in the hot, dusty room all day. Frightened and hungry, she could not get out or signal for help. Bonnie was finally rescued when the neighbors came looking for her in a neighborhood search. Decades later, Bonnie still fears being in a room with a closed door and no windows.[8]*

**Cryophobia**—Imagine how it would be if you lived in northern Minnesota, where the temperature often dips below

While reptiles are certainly not for everybody, some people have an intense fear of the eyes, scales, and tongues of frogs, lizards, and snakes. Batrachophobia is the name of this condition.

zero during the winter, and you had cryophobia. People with cryophobia fear cold or cold objects. They may fear cold weather, being outdoors in the winter, or not being able to stay warm enough during the winter. Sometimes these people will overdress to stay warm. Some people who fear cold avoid adding ice to drinks or drinking cold beverages at all.

**Cyberphobia**—Most of us would have a hard time avoiding computers today. However, some people fear, distrust, or even hate computers. If they are forced to work with computers, they may sweat a lot, become dizzy or nauseated, and have trouble breathing. Their blood pressure skyrockets. Many people with cyberphobia struggle to hide their fears since they must work with computers during school or in their jobs.

**Cynophobia**—Some people do not think that dogs are people's best friends. People with cynophobia fear dogs, perhaps because they remind them of wolves or jackals. Others dislike a dog's smell, fur, barking, or tendency to be noisy and destructive. Many people who have cynophobia find that their fear comes from being bitten or snapped at by a dog when they were children.

**Dental phobia**—Some people fear dentists so much that they would rather suffer severe tooth pain than seek dental help. Therapists find that such a strong fear of dentists can often be traced to a bad dental experience in childhood. Someone with mild dental fear will have a dry mouth, sweaty palms, and a faster than normal heart rate. Those with high dental fear do not breathe well; this alone can bring on light-headedness and increased anxiety. Some people will actually jump out of the dental chair and run out of the room, especially at the sight or sound of the dentist's drill. Those people with strong dental phobia will not seek dental care—sometimes for decades at a time.[9]

**Entomophobia**—An enormous variety of insects inhabit the earth. Unfortunately, some people fear these tiny creatures so much that they can never open their windows. They may even seal the windows shut. They may vacuum and sweep several times a day in hopes of catching any stray insects that wandered into their house or apartment. Some people with entomophobia seldom leave their clean and safe homes for fear of seeing or being touched by an insect. They get their homes fumigated regularly. People sometimes focus on a particular type of insect, such as butterflies or dragonflies, because they are afraid of flying insects. People who have entomophobia often say that they dislike insects so much because they bite, cause itching, or carry disease.

**Eremophobia**—People who never *want* to be alone sometimes *fear* being alone. For some, this fear is worse if they are sick or in pain. Sometimes this fear is wrapped in other fears, such as the fear of becoming old (gerascophobia). Benjamin Rush (1745–1837), a noted American doctor, called eremophobia "solo phobia."

**Gephyrophobia**—People who are afraid to cross bridges actually may fear being trapped. They also may be afraid of being in narrow spaces, or they may fear heights. For people with gephyrophobia, trying to cross a bridge causes them to gasp for breath, break into a sweat, and get weak in the legs so that they cannot walk well. Many cannot cross a bridge, whether on foot or in a bus or car.

**Hemophobia**—Some people feel a bit queasy at the sight of blood. Some look away when they are about to get an injection by a doctor or nurse. For people with hemophobia, the sight or thought of blood causes a deep fear. People with this phobia or injury phobias (traumatophobia) usually go through all the feelings and symptoms of those with other phobias, but with

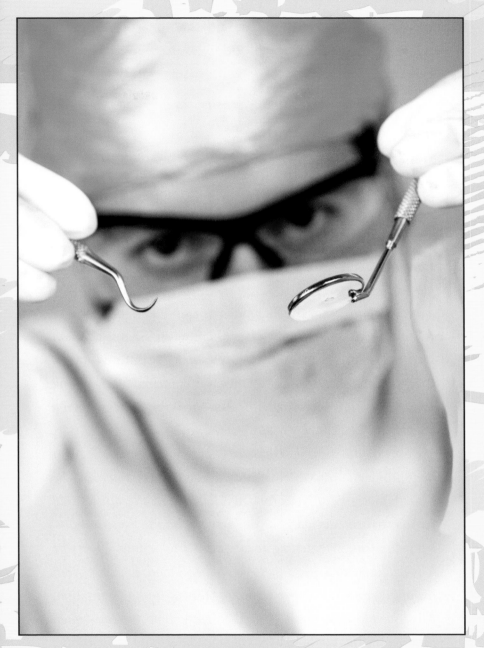

Fear of the dentist is a common occurrence. Dental phobia is an intense fear that keeps sufferers from visiting the dentist—even at the expense of the health of their teeth.

61

one difference: When they are afraid, their heart rate increases, then suddenly drops. Their blood pressure plunges, and often they faint.

*Sarah remembered that while she was in grade school, she would close her eyes during bloody movie scenes. That was not unusual, because other kids did the same thing. However, when she was about sixteen, she saw a newspaper photo of bloody palm prints. She fainted. Sometime later, during a history class movie, she fainted during a bloody scene.*

*Sarah then started fainting once a week. The fainting started to happen twice a week, then every day, until she was fainting every few hours. Sarah remembered, "The Gulf War was going on at that time, so magazines and newspapers were full of bloody images and ideas. In English class, we'd read stories in which people were injured, and those scared me. In biology class, talking about body parts made me faint. I think my imagination was too vivid!" She once even fainted when a teacher gave her back a test corrected with red ink!*

*Sarah's medical tests found nothing unusual. She got help from the Anxiety Disorders Research Center at the State University of New York at Albany. The therapists tried various treatments with Sarah. First, she had to list situations, from the least frightening to the most frightening. Then she learned how to tense up, to keep her blood pressure from dropping, and to keep from fainting during a phobic reaction. Most people with phobias need to learn how to relax when they are afraid, but Sarah had to learn how to do the opposite. She practiced tensing her muscles while standing, sitting, and walking. Finally, the therapists had Sarah choose a piece of cheerful music.*

*Sarah's work on her phobia began. The first thing on her list was to write the word blood many, many times. She practiced her muscle tensing and listened to her favorite music. Soon she was comfortable with writing blood. She then learned to look at raw meat, bloody pictures, and movies without feeling faint. After only three months, she no longer fainted or felt anxious at the sight or thought of blood.*

*"My final tasks were to have my blood drawn and to watch a hip operation. When I went to get my blood drawn, the doctor couldn't find my vein, so he let me draw his blood!" she said. She liked watching the hip operation. "I think the therapist who came along with me was more upset than I was." Now Sarah says she still feels a bit uncomfortable about blood and injuries, but she can handle herself just fine.*[10]

**Lachanophobia**—"Eat your vegetables," mothers often tell their children. Some people, though, are afraid of vegetables. Some people with lachanophobia say that they cannot eat anything that has grown in the ground. Others fear that they are eating contaminated vegetables, because plants absorb pollutants from the water and air.

**Microphobia**—Germs, a general word for tiny organisms that cause disease, refers to bacteria and viruses. In addition to bacteria and viruses, people with microphobia can also fear molds and yeasts. People with microphobia tend to keep themselves and their possessions ultraclean. They may also fear diseases.

**Musicophobia,  melophobia**—Throughout history, certain types of music have been feared and, as a result, banned. For example, Adolf Hitler outlawed any music by Jewish composers during his reign in Germany. For decades, rock and roll music has been feared and disliked by some people.

In the early 1950s, some cities banned rock and roll dances and concerts in public places, dance halls, and at swimming pools. Schools forbade it at dances and shows. During the 1960s, songs by the Beatles and the Rolling Stones were banned by some people because of their lyrics. Rock songs of the 1970s about sex, antiwar protests, and drugs were censored. Censorship of some popular music continues today by disc jockeys, record store owners, politicians, school officials, churches and other special-interest groups, and parents.[11] People with a musicophobia generally fear only one type of music, for example, organ music.

**People with nosemaphobia or nosophobia fear they will come down with a specific disease.**

64

*Erica violently disliked rock music, although she once had liked it a lot. Her fear grew out of a horrible accident. One winter night, she was in a car with four other college students. The road was icy, and the driver lost control of the car and crashed through an embankment, killing four people trapped inside. Only Erica survived. She was stuck inside the car for hours, in terrible pain, with her four dead friends. The only sound she heard was the rock music coming from the car radio.*

*After she was rescued, Erica could no longer listen to rock music, although she had forgotten about the radio playing in the wrecked car. Soon, her dislike of rock music had grown to a phobia, and then it spread to any situations involving rock music such as parties, dances, and concerts.[12]*

**Musophobia, murophobia**—Fear of mice or rats is a well-known and common phobia. People with this phobia say their fear comes from knowing that rodents eat and destroy food. They associate mice and rats with dirt and disease and intensely dislike their small, black droppings. Rat bites can lead to rat-bite fever. This serious disease causes fever, chills, bad headaches, and rashes. Because these animals are small, they can hide in small places. People with musophobia are terrified of mice or rats suddenly scurrying out at them. People who fear mice and rats try to avoid them. If they see one, they scream, jump, or run away from them, or even faint. Most people with musophobia develop their fear as young children.

**Nosemaphobia, nosophobia**—Some people with nosemaphobia or nosophobia worry about catching or having a specific illness or disease. This is different from hypochondria. People suffering from hypochondria are convinced that they are ill or are about to become ill. They worry about minor things like an occasional cough or sneeze. Fear of specific diseases changes over time, depending on what diseases are most common and terrifying. Today, people with nosemaphobia often fear death from: AIDS (Acquired Immune Deficiency Syndrome), cancer, and heart disease. As a result, they avoid anything that may remind them of the disease, including newspaper articles and television and radio programs. They often search their bodies for any signs of the disease and go to doctors for frequent tests. Fear of illness is most common among middle-aged and older persons and occurs in more women than men.

**Numerophobia**—Fear of numbers can take several forms. Some people fear certain numbers such as one or thirteen. (The fear of the number thirteen is called triskaidekaphobia.) Mathematics or working with numbers strikes fear into the hearts of some people. Taking a math test makes some people anxious. Others experience terror if they have to try to figure out a bus timetable or count change. Some people dislike getting numbers assigned to them. Social security numbers, work identification numbers, credit card numbers, even library card numbers can upset a person with numerophobia.

**Nyctophobia**—Young children sometimes fear the night. That is because they fear the unknown, the dark, or being separated from their parents and being alone. Children with nyctophobia imagine monsters under their beds, in their closets, or at their bedroom windows. Sometimes people are afraid that they will not wake up the next morning.

People who do not sleep well sometimes fear the night, especially if they have a hard time falling asleep, wake up during the night, or have nightmares. Nightmares often cause the person to wake up screaming. Luckily, most children outgrow their night terrors.

**Occupational phobias**—People sometimes develop phobias because of their work in dangerous jobs.

*Jim's phobia appeared immediately after his on-the-job accident. Jim, a miner, was at work 4,000 feet underground. A large air current caused his safety helmet to fly into the bottom of an elevator shaft. Jim leaned in to get his helmet. Suddenly, the eight-ton steel elevator cage crashed down and pinned his head against the guardrails. After quite a while, the other miners freed him, and Jim was rushed to the hospital for surgery. He recovered physically, but he continued to have horrible nightmares about being in dark, closed-in places. After six weeks of treatment for his claustrophobia, Jim overcame it.[13]*

Treatment has helped others overcome their occupational phobias, including a construction worker who fell five stories and became afraid of heights (acrophobia, hysophobia), and another man who was badly burned at work and could not stand to be near fire, not even a match (pyrophobia).

**Ochlophobia, demophobia, enochlophobia**—The fear of crowds, which includes fear of being with a large number of people in one place, is probably related to claustrophobia. If they are in a crowd, people with this type of phobia may fear that they cannot get out fast enough, or that there is no place that is safe with so many people around. Many people with agoraphobia also fear crowds.

**Odynophobia**—No one likes or wants to be in pain, but some people develop extreme fears of even mild pain. A person with odynophobia will avoid seeing a doctor or dentist, or going to a hospital. Usually, people with odynophobia worry more about avoiding physical pain than actually experiencing it.

**Ombrophobia**—Gardeners usually hope for rain so that their plants will grow well. People who fear rain will avoid even walking in it. They will check the weather regularly, and they try to avoid being outside when rain is predicted.

**Ophidiophobia**—One of the most common phobias of people throughout the world is of snakes. People cite several reasons for their fear: Snakes can bite them and cause illness; poisonous snakes can give them a fatal snakebite; snakes slither and look slimy; pythons and boa constrictors can crush people to death. Many people cannot tell a poisonous snake from one that is not poisonous. Poisonous snakes, while rare, do live in some parts of the United States.

**Ornithophobia**—People with this phobia often fear that a bird's sudden movements mean that the bird will attack them. Others say that the swooping movements and the sight and sound of flapping wings frighten them. The bird's small, beady eyes and sharp claws scare others. Many people with ornithophobia fear pigeons, since these birds live around buildings and people more than other birds do. Sometimes people only fear dead birds. Keith Schooler, referred to in Chapter 2, remembers when his ornithophobia began. "When I was about four years old, I was in the chicken coop, collecting eggs. Suddenly, all the chickens began running toward me. I felt trapped and scared. I just turned and ran out of there."[14] People with severe ornithophobia fear leaving their houses, walking outside, or traveling by car or bus. They keep all windows tightly closed. In extreme cases, people will not look outside, to avoid seeing any birds.

**Papyrophobia**—A fear of paper can include the fear of touching or seeing paper, being cut by paper edges, or thinking about paper. Any type of paper qualifies: wrapping paper, wallpaper, or drawing paper. Jack had a rare newspaper phobia.

**Birds can instill fear in people. Some are put off by their beaks and beady eyes, while others fear their sudden movements.**

His fear was greater if the newspaper was damp. If he saw some torn, wet newspapers, he would have a phobic attack. A former politician, Jack kept his fear of newspapers a secret because he worried that his political opponents would ridicule him.

Jack said, "Ever since I can remember, I've been afraid to touch or be touched by a newspaper, or even to handle a newspaper clipping. And the sight of a wet paper, or the idea of coming into contact with wet newsprint, makes me nauseous. Sometimes people tap me with a paper and I just about faint." He had no fear of books, magazines, or other types of paper.

He avoided subways, because he was afraid of being brushed by someone carrying a newspaper. If he saw a *newspaper stand or bundles of newspapers, he would race to the other side of the street. Jack has worked on his fear, though. He can now read a newspaper, but he can touch it with only one or two fingers.*[15]

**Public speaking**—Phobias involving public speaking are some of the most widespread phobias in the United States. Also called stage fright or performance anxiety, this fear is actually a form of social phobia. Many people get sweaty hands or butterflies in the stomach in certain situations, particularly before and during public speeches and musical, dramatic, or other performances. This surge of fear, particularly before a performance, is common.

Over time, many people learn how to deal with their fears. Taking deep breaths before going on stage helps, as does positive thinking. Experience with performing or speaking in front of audiences tends to reduce anxieties.

Someone with severe performance anxiety has a persistent, irrational fear of being watched and judged by the audience. This phobia has affected the careers of talented musicians, actors, and other performers. Sometimes they may need help to deal with their phobia. Treatment with antianxiety drugs has been helpful for people such as musicians, public speakers, pilots, and athletes.

**Scolionphobia**—This is school phobia, which usually starts during the grade school years and is equally common in girls and boys. Therapists often find that it is actually an exaggerated fear of leaving the home or parents. Many children display a wide range of symptoms that include headaches, vomiting, diarrhea, stomach pain, feeling faint, and a sore throat. Some may cry a lot. Children with school phobias are

Actor Harrison Ford reportedly has a fear of public speaking. That's not a problem for his famous character Indiana Jones. However, the archaeology professor is afraid of snakes.

often embarrassed about their phobia and tend to avoid their friends.

**Technophobia**—A 2014 Pew Research study revealed that about 3 in 10 Americans were wary of new technology, such as driverless cars, wearable technology, and lab-produced meats. People with technophobia may feel anxious when thinking about current or future technology. They also experience great anxiety and raised blood pressure when faced with using current technology to complete everyday tasks, such as using a computer to shop online, setting a car's GPS system to navigate a route, programming a DVR to record a television show, or figuring out how to use a video chat application to talk to faraway friends and family. Cyberphobia—the fear of computers—is a form of technophobia.

Some people with technophobia fear that machines will replace people. Younger people are generally less likely to have technophobia than older people. "Technology is a sign of our times," said Dan Gookin, author of the several computer and technology books in the . . . For Dummies series. However, he believes, "Technology has simply passed many people by."[16]

**Triskaidekaphobia**—Have you been in any tall buildings without a floor numbered thirteen? Because fear of the number thirteen is so common, some building owners skip this number. People with triskaidekaphobia fear anything involving the number, including apartment or house numbers, phone numbers, or the thirteenth day of the month. "My kindergarten teacher feared the number thirteen," Clay Bartl remembered. "My birthday is December 13, but she had the class celebrate my birthday on December 12. I was only six years old, and didn't understand her phobia. I had to ask my parents why she pretended my birthday was on the twelfth."[17]

**Tropophobia, neophobia**—People who fear moving or making changes generally like routines because they provide security. For some of these people, any changes in their jobs or changes in their routes to and from school or work can cause panic. New jobs or homes are particularly scary to these people. Moving to a new school involves a lot of changes, such as making new friends, getting to know the teachers, finding new clubs or activities, and so on. In extreme cases, people with tropophobia or neophobia will not travel because they fear new places.

**Vermiphobia, scoleciphobia**—People who fear worms avoid going to places where worms are easily seen, such as bait stores, rivers, lakes, or swamps. Some people with this phobia will not go out on rainy days for fear of seeing worms on the sidewalk.

**Xenophobia**—Babies and young children sometimes are afraid of strangers and react by crying or screaming. Researchers find that xenophobia is common from ages six to twelve months. Most of us outgrow this fear, but some people continue to avoid strangers. They also often fear parties and crowds (ochlophobia).

**Zoophobia**—Researchers find that many people fear animals. People with zoophobia fear animals in general, while others fear wild animals (agrizoophobia) or particular animals such as snakes (ophidiophobia) or mice (musophobia). These phobias often develop while a child is young, from age four to eight. An attack by a rat, a dog bite, a scary movie about sharks such as *Jaws*, or hearing someone scream in reaction to a snake may start a young child on the path toward an animal phobia. Sometimes adults develop animal phobias as well.

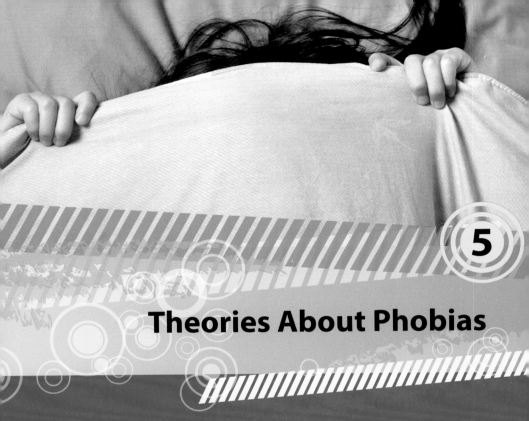

**5**

# Theories About Phobias

It is not known what causes phobias, although researchers have come up with several theories to explain them. Researchers developed these theories by observing and listening to patients, and by measuring and recording patients' reactions in laboratory settings. Once researchers come up with a theory, they test them through experiments. Researchers have so far found that the underlying causes of phobias are often complex. Theories about phobias fall into five categories: psychological, conditioned, biological, cultural, or a combination of theories.

## Psychological Theories About Phobias

Some researchers have concluded that phobias arise when people ignore problems and conflicts. For example, if someone has a stressful home life and never gets help, then that person's

75

anxiety will grow. Over time, that anxiety can grow into a phobia. The phobia is the way that person manages the anxiety-producing situation. The phobia allows the person to focus all of his or her anxiety onto one situation or thing, rather than addressing the underlying problem. Here is how this type of phobia developed for one person:

> *A medical student always felt anxious when he took the subway to his classes. One day, he got angry with a professor during a class and stormed out. The next day, he stopped at the wide, busy street near the school but could not walk across it because he felt afraid. He got home by taking a subway and a taxi, so he did not have to walk across any streets. After that, this young man could not leave his home: He had developed agoraphobia. When he sought help, his therapist discovered that this man had never wanted to become a doctor; that it had been his parents' dream for him. Family therapy resulted in three things: The young man left medical school, he returned to college, and he earned a degree in sociology, which was his real interest.[1]*

One woman who could not leave her home realized during therapy that her agoraphobia had started after she was charged with shoplifting. For other people, agoraphobia often follows a severe shock, such as the death of a husband, wife, or close friend, or after a major event, such as surgery.

Social phobias often develop from complex causes. Some people with social phobias describe being overly concerned about others' opinions. Many people with social phobias become overly concerned about terrible things happening that are and beyond their control.[2] This theory may explain why a death or major surgery may trigger agoraphobia. It also explains why some people with agoraphobia can leave their homes if a trusted person (a husband, wife, child, or close friend) goes out with them.

Some psychologists believe that phobias result when serious issues are left unaddressed. Acknowledgement and proper management of traumatic situations may lessen the development of phobias.

*At age 40, Mrs. M. first began having panic attacks, which then developed into agoraphobia. She quit her job and would not leave her home for years. She focused her energies on worrying about her healthy, hardworking husband. Perhaps her agoraphobia started when Mrs. M. was a young child. Dr. Julian M. Herskowitz, director of an anxiety treatment clinic called TERRAP in Huntington, New York, stated, "Overprotective parents can project their own fears onto the child and give them the feeling that the world is a dangerous place where anything bad can happen at any time. And when a spouse becomes overly concerned about the other partner, that is often an indication that the worry is really about oneself, about being left alone."[3]*

## Biological Theories About Phobias

Other researchers theorize that body chemistry leads people to develop phobias. Some researchers have found that people who have phobias have lower than normal levels of the chemical dopamine in their brains.

Researchers have found can cause panic attacks in some people by injecting them with certain chemicals, such as sodium lactate. After they have had one panic attack, they were more likely to have them again if they were injected with the same chemicals. Some people with agoraphobia appear to have unusual brain chemistry and react differently to stress than do people who do not have the phobia. These people were also found to be sensitive to some chemicals, such as caffeine. This drug is in coffee, tea, chocolate, hot cocoa, and many soft drinks.

Dr. Harold Levinson offers another theory. In his book *Phobia Free*, he writes that 90 percent of all phobias are caused by physical problems with the inner ear. He reports that medication for inner ear disorders, used with therapy, has helped many of his patients.

Other researchers say that some people may have inherited a genetic predisposition to phobias. This means genes that can transmit certain characteristics were passed on from the parents to their children. No one knows what causes the phobia to grow in some people, but not in others.[4] Arthur Henley, in his book, *Phobias: The Crippling Fears*, writes, "Theoretically, all of us may harbor a phobia 'germ' but in most of us it will remain dormant because something in our nature keeps it quiescent [quiet]."[5]

Genetic researchers have studied families to find out if heredity can determine who will develop phobias. Their studies show that certain phobias often run in families, especially agoraphobia and some specific phobias. A Norwegian study found that identical twins were more likely to have social phobias in common than were fraternal twins. One researcher has found that people with relatives who have phobias are two to three times more likely to develop phobias themselves.[6] However, researchers cannot tell if this tendency is inherited or if it is learned by growing up around or living with someone with a phobia. Although paralyzing fears can run in families, family members also can help each other overcome fears.

Some people with social phobia remember that they were easily scared when they were children, at age four or five. They hid from relatives who came to their homes, or they could not speak in class. Another trait many people with social phobia share is great sensitivity to rejection.

## Conditioning Theories About Phobias

Some researchers say that people learn fear through direct experience. Specific phobias sometimes develop from a scary

Fear of dogs does not usually arise out of nowhere. Often, the phobia stems from experiencing or learning about a scary experience with a dog.

situation or real danger. For example, a person who is thrown from a horse may develop an intense fear of horses. If a child sees someone bitten by a snake or is continually warned to be careful of snakes, then the child may learn to fear snakes.

In the 1920s, J. B. Watson (1878–1958), an American psychologist, trained a young boy to fear rats (musophobia). Whenever a white rat was placed by the child, a loud noise blared. After a while, the boy screamed when any rat appeared. His phobia grew to dogs, rabbits, and even a piece of cotton. Some researchers claim that Watson's cruel experiment shows that incorrect learning or conditioning can often result in a phobia.

Larry L. King (1929–2012), a playwright, wrote about how he developed cynophobia (fear of dogs). Until he was nearly three, King and his beloved dog, Shep, happily played together. Then Shep got rabies. Two men came to King's house and shot and killed his dog. The terrible memories of his pet's death remained in his mind, and King started to fear all dogs. At age eight, after he was viciously attacked by two large neighborhood dogs, he began to have nightmares about dogs. He arranged elaborate routes to get home from school so he could avoid any dogs. King's dog phobia continued until he was married, with two children. King's mother-in-law asked him to look after Bandit, her small dog. Embarrassed to admit his phobia, King agreed. During a long afternoon, gentle Bandit reminded King that dogs can be fun and can provide good company. King was finally able to overcome his phobia and welcome a dog into his family home.[7]

Therapists point out, though, that not everyone who is attacked by a dog develops a dog phobia. Other people who never are hurt by a bird may develop a bird phobia after seeing a scary movie about birds.

81

## Cultural Theories About Phobias

Another group of researchers point to culture as the cause of phobias. They think that the way people live, as well as the people, customs, and beliefs they grow up learning about, cause certain people to develop phobias. Cultures that allow people to express their fears and worries freely develop tend to have fewer people with phobias than do cultures that insist that people hide their feelings. Some research has shown that there appear to be few phobias in Mediterranean cultures (such as Italian, Spanish, and Greek). These are all cultures that encourage people to display and discuss their feelings.[8]

**Phobias are not as common in Mediterranean cultures, such as Greece. This may be because the people of these cultures are encouraged to confront and express their feelings.**

Phobias are common in childhood and the existence of childhood phobias is nearly universal across cultures.[9] Some researchers find that certain fears have always been known to people of all ages, throughout the centuries, across cultures. These universal phobias include the fear of snakes, mice, insects, and knives—potentially dangerous things that people usually have some apprehension about but which for some people develops into a phobia.

## A Mixture of Causes

Researchers have performed many experiments to determine the cause of phobias. No single theory has proven to be correct, however. Many researchers tend to think that specific phobias come from early experience and learning. Agoraphobia, and some social phobias, seem to stem from biological causes. Most likely, all phobias develop from some combination of psychological, biological, conditioned, and cultural causes.

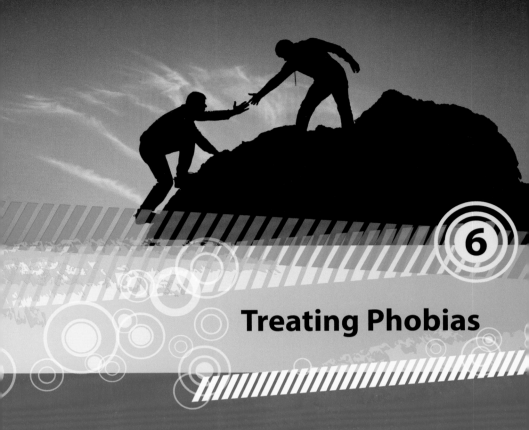

**6**

# Treating Phobias

While the causes of many phobias may still remain mysterious, they can be effectively treated. The Anxiety and Depression Association of America reports that most people with anxiety disorders, including phobias, recover or see significant progress after undergoing some form of treatment for their disorder.[1] However, they also report that only about one-third of people with anxiety or a phobia seek treatment.[2]

The type of treatment varies for each person's case and can include sessions with therapists, medication, self-help, and combinations of therapies. Treatment periods vary from a few months to a year or more. Most treatments focus on helping people cope with their phobic reactions so that they can control their fears and lead a fuller, happier life.

For most people with phobias, there is a typical cycle of fear and tension. First, there is the situation or thing they fear, followed by the actions they take to avoid what they fear, and then an attempt to ignore the tension created by their fear and avoidance. People with phobias need to break their fear cycle. Some people can do this by themselves or with the help of a support group. Other people may need different types of treatment.

## Mason's Driving Phobia

*Mason kept his fear of driving a secret from other people for many years. His was afraid of being humiliated. He worried that he could not parallel park, or would drive too slowly and make someone angry, or panic and lose control of his car and kill someone. "I couldn't stand being exposed as a failure. My heart would pound, I would get very nervous, and I would start to lock up whenever I even thought about driving," he said.[3]*

*"Most people think I must have had a bad experience driving when I was younger, but the truth is I was 32 years old before I ever got behind a wheel!" Mason finally got tired of making excuses and trying to find someone to drive him places. He decided that he needed to learn to drive. "I couldn't face the humiliation of asking one of my friends to teach me, so I signed up with one of those big driving schools. I figured if I couldn't stand the driving lessons, I would just quit. You know, just fade away quietly."[4]*

*At first, Mason tried to postpone his lessons, and he made all kinds of excuses to his instructor. The instructor kept pestering Mason to try. Mason said, "Finally, I had to give in and make an appointment or let my instructor know I was a real coward." Mason did go on to get his license. "Now I can actually talk openly about my fear of driving, acknowledge it, but not give in to it."[5]*

Acknowledging that you have a fear will allow others to understand and help you. Ignoring a problem can result in making it worse, and it can prevent you from living your best life.

Many people with phobias go to great lengths to work around their fears and never deal directly with them. At some point in their life, some, like Mason, decide to fight their fears by themselves. Others may need professional help to reduce their stress and anxiety and build their self-esteem. This knowledge can help people with phobias. Therapists and treatment programs also offer people individual or group treatments.

## Self-Help

Today people can go online or to any bookstore or public library to find self-help books and workbooks on dealing with phobias and panic attacks. Some people work through the books by themselves. Others use them with a therapist.

Some people are able help themselves by lowering their overall tension level. Their endless fear cycle increases their everyday tension and damages their self-esteem. By lowering their tension, they lessen the chance that they will panic or have a phobic reaction. The methods listed below are all ways that can help people better handle panic attacks and phobic reactions.

***Relaxation or meditation.*** Studies show that relaxation and meditation cause chemical changes in the brain, which produces a feeling of peace and acceptance. These feelings are calming to someone with a phobia. Regular, deep breathing is a key aid, as is relaxing the muscles to lessen tension. People perform deep breathing and relaxing exercises before or during a phobic reaction. There are many self-help books and workbooks, television shows, DVDs, audiobooks, and classes that teach relaxation or meditation. Therapists often teach these techniques, too.

***Positive imagery.*** People use reassuring, positive images and memories to relax themselves, which helps ward off phobic reactions. There are many self-help books, DVDs, and audiobooks that teach people about positive imagery. The technique is easy to learn.

*Physical exercise*. People who are constantly anxious build up nervous tension. The body can release this energy through regular exercise, and this helps people deal with phobias. Physical exercise builds confidence, self-esteem, and a healthy feeling. Probably the easiest exercise that uses the large muscles of the body is walking. Swimming, jogging, bicycling, skating, tennis—any regular exercise will also give the mind and body a boost.

*Learn acceptance*. Experts say that people with phobias should not fight their feelings and fears. Acceptance helps people gain control over their phobias. Instead of negative self-talk such as "I look foolish" or "Everyone sees me sweating," people learn to substitute positive or accepting self-messages. Before phobic feelings develop, people can say things to themselves such as:

> *I look good today.*
>
> *My class report is interesting.*

If they feel a phobic reaction building, they can say positive, reassuring things such as:

> *I'm going to think slowly about this.*
>
> *I don't like feeling this way, but I can accept it.*
>
> *I can feel like this and still be OK.*
>
> *This has happened before and I was OK. I'll be OK this time, too.*[6]

*Don't self-medicate*. Therapists recommend that people with a history of anxiety, including phobias, reduce their caffeine. Dr. Edmund Bourne, a psychologist who specializes in treating anxiety, advises that most people prone to anxiety or panic should keep their "total caffeine consumption to less than 100 mg [milligram]/day. For example, one cup of percolated coffee or two diet cola beverages a day would be a maximum. For those people who are very sensitive to caffeine, less than 50 mg/day would be advisable."[7] But perhaps eliminating caffeine altogether would be a good step to take.

Another way to reduce anxiety is to stop using alcohol, and tobacco. Some people try to manage their fears by drinking. However, using alcohol in this way may increase phobic

**Using drugs and alcohol as a way to cope with a problem will not solve it. In fact, it most likely will add to your problems.**

episodes and may lead to alcoholism. Nicotine, the drug found in tobacco, can cause anxiety. Illegal drugs, including marijuana, cocaine, and heroin, can produce excessive anxiety and other phobic symptoms.

## Learning Skills

People need to know how to succeed at work and at school, handle stress, make and keep friends, succeed in marriage, raise children, and so on. Some people never learned or developed these social and coping skills.

Various places offer low-cost skill training classes or seminars, including continuing education programs at colleges and universities, community colleges, junior colleges, community mental health centers, community education centers, health maintenance organizations (HMOs), churches, hospitals, and many training institutions. Community education centers often offer teen programs, too.

These skill-training classes go by many names, including assertiveness training, self-esteem building, stress management, relaxation training, and grief and loss programs. These classes and seminars are advertised in local newspapers, class catalogs, clinic waiting rooms, community and church bulletins, and can be researched online.

## National Organizations

There are organizations throughout the United States that offer education about phobias and also provide referrals to mental health treatment professionals, self-help groups, and other local resources.

***Anxiety and Depression Association of America (ADAA)***—Founded in 1980, this national organization in Silver Spring, Maryland, aids people with phobias and their families through education and information. ADAA publishes a variety of materials for people with phobias and also for health professionals who are treating those with phobias. ADAA does not recommend any one treatment and encourages people to check around and find what works best for the individual. This organization's website includes an information database on phobias and other anxiety disorders and provides a list of mental health professionals. The ADAA also operates a self-help network for locating local support groups.

*Mental Health America (MHA)*—This group was founded in by Clifford W. Beers in 1909 and is headquartered in Alexandria, Virginia. The MHA Web site provides information on phobias and lists of mental health organizations that provide resources and information about self-help groups, treatment professionals, and community clinics. MHA also works with the federal government to promote research and services for those people with mental health problems.

*The National Institutes of Mental Health (NIMH)*—The National Institutes of Mental Health is part of the United States Department of Health and Human Services. It is headquartered in Rockville, Maryland, and is the world's largest research organization that specializes in studying mental illness. Its website provides information about mental illness, and lists resources for finding help.

## Finding Support or Self-Help Groups

Support and self-help groups can be found throughout the United States. These organizations offer alternatives to therapy or can be used in addition to therapy. These groups usually consist of people with phobias or other anxiety disorders and sometimes their families. The groups help members learn and share experiences.

***Agoraphobics in Motion (AIM)***—Since 1983, AIM has offered support to people with agoraphobia and related anxiety problems. This self-help program has three locations in Michigan. People can sign up for small group discussions and support, field trips, and relaxation technique courses.

***Agoraphobics Building Independent Lives (ABIL)*** is a network of support groups for people with agoraphobia and other phobias and panic-related disorders. Formed in 1986, ABIL is not affiliated with any religious organization, nor is it a therapy group. Instead, it offers members a place to set goals

Speaking with others who share the same or similar fears in a support group will help you address your phobia. It also helps to know that you are not alone.

to overcome problems, share successes, and learn how to deal with setbacks.

*Recovery International*—Started in Chicago in 1937 by Dr. Abraham A. Low, Recovery International has grown to include support groups throughout the United States. Groups also meet in Canada and Ireland. Recovery International teaches people to deal with their phobic reactions through weekly support group meetings. This program helps people deal with crises, fears, panic, and anxiety. It emphasizes taking responsibility for oneself and learning self-confidence.

Recovery International offers no medical advice and advises people to follow their doctors' instructions. No professionals are involved, and Recovery is not affiliated with any organizations or religion. One group leader explained, "We have limitations—no diagnosing, no counseling, and no giving advice at the meeting."[8] Held in a public place such as a library, church, or YMCA, each meeting opens with a reading or a taped lecture. Members then tell about using the Recovery method during the week. They also describe how they would have reacted before learning Recovery's methods. A question and comment period follows, and then members break into small groups for discussion.

## Seeking Therapy

Therapists tailor treatment for each person. No one treatment works for all phobias, and people may want to try different ones. The length of treatment depends on the person, the phobia, and the treatment. Some people overcome their phobias in a few weeks, while others take months or longer. To determine if a treatment is helping, the ADAA advises that people should see some improvement within 12 to 16 weeks. Most people do not go into a hospital for treatment; they visit a therapist's office for treatment sessions.[9]

When treating people with phobias, therapists generally use a combination of behavior therapy, cognitive therapy, and relaxation therapy. Behavior therapy helps people with phobias change and gain control over their unwanted behaviors. This therapy emphasizes that people change their behaviors based on knowledge they learn about themselves. Behavior therapists often teach people to cope by guiding them through exposure to feared situations or objects. Because people work on their own recovery, they develop skills that they can use after therapy ends. In cognitive therapy, which was developed in the 1960s, people first analyze their feelings. They learn to separate realistic and unrealistic thoughts, then change their thought patterns. The goal is to change self-defeating or distorted thoughts.

***Relaxation therapy*** includes various techniques. Deep breathing probably ranks as the most important. People learn to breathe slowly and deeply from the diaphragm. This helps during periods of "fight or flight" because breathing tends to become shallow and rapid, which adds to panic. People also find progressive relaxation of the body's muscle groups relaxing. Thinking of calming thoughts or repeating a simple word or phrase may also help ward off a panic attack. Yoga can also be employed as a form of relaxation therapy.

Many therapists combine behavior and cognitive therapy, along with relaxation training, when treating phobias. The goal in behavior therapy is for the person actually to confront the feared situation or object and to learn that nothing horrible happens. To do this, the person goes through a series of graded steps, often beginning with an imagined step, then continuing through successive steps to the real situation itself. Cognitive therapy, used with behavior therapy, teaches people to quiet

Seeking treatment from an experienced therapist can help you overcome your fears. They will listen to your problems and devise a plan to work through or manage your phobias.

the thoughts that feed the phobia. These therapies are used once a week for 10 to 24 sessions.

Here is an example of how combined therapy works. Arthur Decker, a licensed psychologist in St. Paul, Minnesota, has provided therapy for many people since 1980.

> "Self-talk in dealing with phobias is important. Instead of panicking, I teach each person that 'I have options.' I help people find the base of their fears, then look at reality and what is rational and what is irrational. Ultimately, I have them face their fears, and do whatever they're afraid of doing. For example, a person came to me for help because of his social phobia. A social phobia is an intense fear of not knowing what to say or do with strangers. This person was beyond shy. He was afraid of being with people and couldn't push himself into social situations.
>
> I had him draw up a list from one to ten of what he considered a little fearful all the way up to frightening. He would try to carry out each step over ten weeks. Meantime, I helped him build on his success by starting small, with nothing overwhelming. The first week he said 'Hi' to a co-worker. Over time, he took a class, then attended an anxiety-phobia group. I taught him how to relax before and after each of these key events. He also learned deep breathing and muscle relaxation. Finally, he achieved his goal—he went to a party."[10]

## Taking Medication

Medications must be prescribed by a doctor and they generally are used only for people with severe phobias. The ADAA stresses that medication must be used along with other forms of therapy. Arthur Decker points out, "Medications can help some people, but they are not a cure-all. Even if you use medications, ninety percent of the time you still have the phobia."[11]

In the early 1960s, researchers discovered that some antidepressants could prevent the panic attacks of agoraphobia. Although scientists are not certain how these drugs work, the idea is that once panic attacks are gone, the person with agoraphobia will be less anxious and start to recover.

Today, doctors prescribe three types of drugs for people with severe phobias: antidepressants, beta-blockers, and antianxiety drugs. Some people find that after six to twelve months they may only need to take medication when they feel particularly anxious, or may even be able to stop taking their medication entirely.[12]

Antidepressants known as elective serotonin reuptake inhibitors (SSRIs) are commonly prescribed to people with panic disorders and phobias. Researchers find that some people who have panic attacks have low serotonin levels. The brain's nerve cells use serotonin as a chemical messenger to transmit information back and forth. If serotonin levels are low, nerve cells misfire or slow down. SSRIs keep the right amount of serotonin in the brain by preventing the body from reabsorbing it. SSRIs affect only serotonin; they do not change other brain chemicals. These drugs include fluoxetine (Prozac), sertraline (Zoloft), paroxetine (Paxil), escitalopram (Lexapro), and venlafaxine (Effexor).

Older classes of antidepressants are tricyclics and monoamine oxidase inhibitors (MAOIs) are prescribe less often because they can react badly with common foods and over-the-counter drugs.

Antianxiety drugs are usually prescribe for shorter periods of time than antidepressants, because people can develop a dependency on them. Common antianxiety drugs include

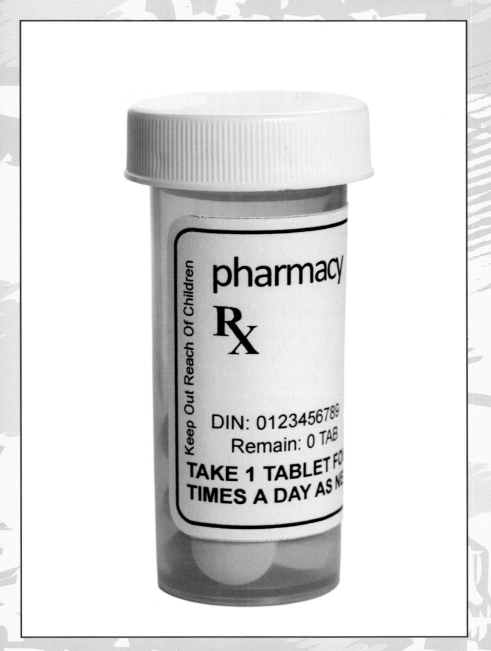

While some fears can be managed through techniques such as relaxation and behavioral modifications, others may be treated with medication.

clonazepam (Klonopin), lorazepam (Ativan), Buspirone (Buspar), and alprazolam (Xanax).

Beta-blockers are drugs created to treat heart conditions. They can also be used to treat anxiety or phobias because they can control the physical symptoms of panic attacks. Beta-blockers might be prescribed to someone who has a phobia that is specific to a certain situation, such as giving a speech.[13]

Prescription drugs can be a useful tool in dealing with anxiety and phobias because they calm physical symptoms, enabling patients to deal with the underlying cause of their fears. However, these drugs can only be prescribed by a medical professional and should only be used as instructed.

## Finding Treatment Programs

There are various programs that are nationally recognized for their treatments. While each has its own method, a typical program involves people with phobias working together in groups with a trained group leader. During the group sessions, people learn new attitudes and skills to help them overcome their phobias.

Each person also has a weekly practice session, either alone or in a group, with a therapist. During these sessions, the person uses the new coping skills in situations that they formerly avoided. Sometimes the therapist stays with the person during these situations. When setbacks occur, more practice is needed.

Although these programs have helped people with phobias across the United States, not everyone can easily get to them. To find therapists or treatment programs in your area, visit the websites of the National Institute of Mental Health, the American Psychiatric Association, Mental Health America, or the ADAA. The "For More Information" section in the back of this book may also be helpful.

**TERRAP (TERRitorial APprehension)** was founded in 1962 by Dr. Arthur B. Hardy. Located in Huntington, New York, it focuses on the causes and treatment of anxieties, fears, and phobias, especially agoraphobia. TERRAP provides information and counseling for those with phobias through group education and treatment manuals. Professionals run the meetings. The treatment manual contains an 18-week course of exercises to teach patients how to manage anxiety.

**Freedom From Fear (FFF)** was established in Staten Island, New York, in 1984. This nonprofit mental illness advocacy organization. It has a treatment and research center in Staten Island, in New York City that aids and counsels people with phobias, fears, depression, and anxieties.

**Midwest Center for Stress and Anxiety** was founded in 1983 by Lucinda Bassett after she overcame her social phobia, as well as her fears of driving and flying. She has developed a fifteen-week home study program that has been used by many people worldwide. There are also self-help podcasts and DVDs available. The Midwest Center is located in Los Angeles, California.

**The Anxiety and Phobia Treatment Center at White Plains Hospital** in New York offers various treatments for people with anxiety and phobias. People can attend Phobia self-help groups. These groups meet regularly for 90 minutes each week and are run by trained phobia aides. For those who can travel to and stay in the White Plains-area for one to two weeks, the center offers an Intensive Course. All treatments focus on helping people deal with their fears through cognitive behavioral therapy. The center was started in 1971.

A phobia aide at the center described how he helped one man overcome his fear of vacations. He had been assigned to work with a famous professor who taught at a graduate school.

Some fears are relatively mild, but others are so intense that only a professional can help. Speak with someone you trust about seeking help for your fears.

While on vacation, the professor awoke from a nap aboard a yacht and had the first phobic reaction of his life. "When he opened his eyes he saw, only two inches from his nose, the bottom of the bunk above his. He felt smothered, trapped and he panicked. Heart pounding, sweating, and trembling, he raced out on deck, breathing hard and struggling for breath."[14]

The professor returned to work, and months passed without any more incidents. Then, while he was on vacation at Disney World in Florida, the professor had another phobic reaction while he was in a plastic bubble ride. He became terrified and climbed right over people to get out of the bubble. Although his phobia did not interfere with his work, he started to worry about traveling on a boat, or airplane, or in a crowded car. He came to the center for treatment.

The phobia aide had a problem carrying out the treatment for the professor. "We could not find a place to practice in which he had fear levels," he explained.[15] The professor needed to learn how to control his fear in the same or similar situations. Then the aide remembered that the professor described his phobia as feeling as if he were in a coffin. He asked the professor if being in the trunk of a closed car would cause him to feel the phobic reactions. The professor said "yes," and treatment started.

While undergoing treatment at the clinic, the professor learned skills that enabled him to manage his fears. Little by little, during each treatment session, the aide was able to close the trunk lid a little more. After eight weeks of treatment, the professor had no problem getting into the trunk and letting the aide shut the trunk completely. During treatment, the professor learned new skills that he could use to handle his fears. Meanwhile, during each treatment session, he allowed

Silverman to close the trunk lid a little more, until it was shut. The professor has enjoyed phobia-free vacations ever since.[16]

## Successful Treatments

While things may not seem hopeful in the middle of a panic attack, chances are good that a person can find a treatment to successfully manage anxiety and phobias. There is a wide variety of help available, including different forms of self-help, medication, and therapy. Once a person finds a treatment or combination of treatments that suits his or her phobia or anxiety, there is a good chance of success. More information is available in the "For More Information" section of this book.

# Chapter Notes

## Chapter 1: Irrational Fears

1. "A Teenager's Struggle With Panic Disorder," *Quest: A Newsletter of the Council on Anxiety Disorders*, Summer 1994, p. 2; Linda Robbian, "The Effect of Panic Disorder on Two High School Students," *Quest: A Newsletter of the Council on Anxiety Disorders*, Fall 1994, pp. 1–2.

2. Joe Eltgroth, personal interview, St. Paul, Minn., August 23, 1994.

3. Harry Milt, *Phobias: The Ailments and the Treatments,* Public Affairs Committee, New York, 1987, pp. 2–3.

4. National Institute of Mental Health, "Any Anxiety Disorder Among Adults," *National Institute of Mental Health,* n.d., <http://www.nimh.nih.gov/health/statistics/prevalence/any-anxiety-disorder-among-adults.shtml> (June 17, 2015).

5. National Institute of Mental Health, "NIMH: Facts About Phobias," *Psych Central,* n.d., <http://psychcentral.com/lib/facts-about-phobias/000658> (February 6, 2015).

6. Life Skills Education, *You & Your Phobias,* Life Skills Education, Northfield, Minn., 1992, p. 4; American Psychiatric Association, "Phobias," *American Psychiatric Association,* 2014, <http://www.psychiatry.org/phobias> (February 5, 2015).

7. Susan Chollar, "Fear Itself," *Woman's Day*, May 18, 1993, p. 68.

8. Jerilyn Ross, *Triumph Over Fear* (New York: Bantam Books, 2009), xvii.

## Chapter 2: Disruptive Phobias

1. Susan Chollar, "Fear Itself," *Woman's Day*, May 18, 1993, p. 70.
2. Amanda Warren, "Scare Tactics: Living With Your Secret Fears," *Mademoiselle*, October 1991, p. 98.
3. Cathy Perlmutter, "5 Who Conquered Fear," *Prevention*, July 1992, p. 105.
4. American Psychiatric Association, "Phobias," *American Psychiatric Association*, 2014, <http://www.psychiatry.org/phobias> (February 5, 2015).
5. Joan W. Anderson, "High Anxiety," *Ladies Home Journal*, February 1992, p. 100.
6. Keith Schooler, personal interview, St. Paul, Minn., August 23, 1994.
7. Stephen Garber, Marianne Garber, and Robyn Spizman, *Monsters Under the Bed and Other Childhood Fears* (New York: Villard Books, 2011), p. 175.
8. Jerilyn Ross, *Triumph Over Fear* (New York: Bantam Books, 2009), pp. 36–37.
9. Ibid., p. 34.
10. American Psychiatric Association, "Phobias," *American Psychiatric Association*, 2014, <http://www.psychiatry.org/phobias> (February 5, 2015).
11. American Psychiatric Association, *Let's Talk Facts About Phobias* (brochure), *American Psychiatric Association*, 2005, <http://www.psychiatry.org/phobias> (February 5, 2015).
12. Jack Maser, "Anxiety Disorders—America's Most Common Mental Health Problem," *ON TARGET: Newsletter of Freedom From Fear, Inc.*, Spring 1994, p. 1; Lesley Jane Seymour, "Fear of Almost Everything," *Mademoiselle*, September 1993, p. 252.
13. American Psychiatric Association, "Phobias," *American Psychiatric Association*, 2014, <http://www.psychiatry.org/phobias> (February 5, 2015).

14. American Psychiatric Association, "Phobias," *American Psychiatric Association,* 2014, <http://www.psychiatry.org/phobias> (February 5, 2015).
15. Carol Schatz, "Drive Me Crazy," *Mademoiselle,* October 1991, p. 100.
16. The Institute for Phobic Awareness, *From Anxiety Addict to Serenity Seeker: Interpreting and Working the 12 Steps of Phobics Anonymous* (Palm Springs, Calif.: The Institute for Phobic Awareness, 1993), p. 42.
17. Anxiety Disorders Association of America, *Phobias,* Anxiety Disorders Association of America, Rockville, Md., 1991, p. 5.
18. The Institute for Phobic Awareness, pp. 164, 165.
19. Mark S. Gold, *The Good News About Panic, Anxiety, and Phobias* (New York: Bantam Books, 1989), p. 37.
20. Carol Schatz, "Fear of Almost Everything," *Mademoiselle,* September 1993, p. 252.
21. Gold, p. 39.
22. Ibid., pp. 11–12.
23. Gold, p. 39.
24. "Cat People," *Catnip,* Tufts University School of Veterinary Medicine Newsletter, July 1994, p. 8.
25. Gold, p. 39
26. Ronald M. Doctor and Ada P. Kahn, *The Encyclopedia of Phobias, Fears, and Anxieties* (New York: Facts on File, 2008), p. 198.
27. Fraser Kent, *Nothing to Fear: Coping With Phobias,* (Garden City, N.Y.: Doubleday, 1977), pp. 6–7.

## Chapter 3: The History of Phobias

1. Fraser Kent, *Nothing to Fear: Coping With Phobias* (Garden City, N.Y.: Doubleday, 1977), p. 11.

2. Ronald M. Doctor and Ada P. Kahn, *The Encyclopedia of Phobias, Fears, and Anxieties* (New York: Facts on File, 2008), p. 312.
3. Ibid., p. 313.
4. Ibid.
5. Lesley Jane Seymour, "Fear of Almost Everything," *Mademoiselle*, September 1993, pp. 252–253; American Psychiatric Association, "DSM-5," *American Psychiatric Association,* 2013, <http://www.psychiatry.org/practice/dsm/dsm5> (February 5, 2015).

## Chapter 4: The Most Common Phobias

1. Fraser Kent, *Nothing to Fear: Coping With Phobias* (Garden City, NY: Doubleday, 1977), pp. 71–72.
2. Hillary Michael Quinn, "Fright Flight," *Mademoiselle*, October 1991, p. 101.
3. Ronald M. Doctor and Ada P. Kahn, *The Encyclopedia of Phobias, Fears, and Anxieties* (New York: Facts on File, 2008), p. 12.
4. Kent, pp. 36–37
5. Carol Murray, personal interview, Little Canada, Minn., October 10, 1994.
6. Tony Whitehead, *Fears and Phobias: What They Are and How to Overcome Them* (New York: Arco, 1983), p. 23.
7. Ibid., pp. 22–23.
8. Bonnie Leir, personal interview, St. Paul, Minn., August 12, 1994.
9. Doctor and Kahn, p. 128; WebMD, "Easing Dental Fear in Adults," *WebMD,* May 22, 2014, <http://www.webmd.com/oral-health/easing-dental-fear-adults> (February 5, 2015).
10. Cathy Perlmutter, "5 Who Conquered Fear," *Prevention*, July 1992, pp. 107–109.

11. Judy Monroe, *Censorship* (New York: Macmillan, 1990), pp. 16–18.

12. Harry Milt, *Phobias: The Ailments and the Treatments,* Public Affairs Committee, New York, 1980, pp. 18–19.

13. Kent, pp. 75–76.

14. Keith Schooler, personal interview, St. Paul, Minn., October 19, 1994.

15. Kent, pp. 77–78.

16. Robert S. Boyd, "Technophobia May Prove Pothole on the Information Superhighway," *St. Paul Pioneer Press*, May 8, 1994, pp. 1A, 11A; T. A. Frail, "New Poll Reveals Americans' Predictions of the Future," *Smithsonian Magazine,* April 17, 2014, <http://www.smithsonianmag.com/arts-culture/new-poll-reveals-americans-predictions-future-180951117/?no-ist> (February 15, 2015).

17. Clay Bartl, personal interview, South St. Paul, Minn., October 29, 1994.

## Chapter 5: Theories About Phobias

1. Tony Whitehead, *Fears and Phobias: What They Are and How to Overcome Them* (New York: Arco, 1983), pp. 34–35.

2. Psych Central, "Separation Anxiety Disorder Symptoms," *Psych Central,* n.d., <http://psychcentral.com/disorders/separation-anxiety-disorder-symptoms/> (February 10, 2015); Psych Central, "Agoraphobia Symptoms," *Psych Central,* n.d., <http://psychcentral.com/disorders/agoraphobia-symptoms/> (February 10, 2015).

3. Arthur Henley, *Phobias: The Crippling Fears* (New York: Avon Books, 1987), pp. 28–29.

4. Marilyn Gellis, personal interview, Palm Springs, Calif., May 28, 1994.

5. Henley, p. 49.

6. Lesley Jane Seymour, "Fear of Almost Everything," *Mademoiselle*, September 1993, p. 254.

7. Larry L. King, "Thanks, Buster," *Parade Magazine,* May 8, 1994, pp. 18–19.

8. Life Skills Education, *You & Your Phobias,* Life Skills Education, Northfield, Minn., 1992, p. 9.

9. Midwest Health Institute, *Phobias,* [audiocassette], (Minneapolis, Minn.: Midwest Health Institute, 1990).

## Chapter 6: Treating Phobias

1. Anxiety and Depression Association of America, "Treatment," *Anxiety and Depression Association of America,* n.d., <http://www.adaa.org/understanding-anxiety/specific-phobias/treatment> (February 10, 2015).

2. Anxiety and Depression Association of America, "Facts and Statistics," *Anxiety and Depression Association of America,* n.d.,<http://www.adaa.org/about-adaa/press-room/facts-statistics> (February 10, 2015).

3. Mark S. Gold, *The Good News About Panic, Anxiety, and Phobias* (New York: Bantam Books, 1989), p. 246.

4. Ibid., pp. 246–247.

5. Ibid., p. 247.

6. Life Skills Education, *You & Your Phobias,* Life Skills Education, Northfield, Minn., 1992, pp. 11–12.

7. Edmund J. Bourne, "Caffeine," *ON TARGET: Newsletter of Freedom from Fear, Inc.,* May 4, 1994, p. 7; Edmund J. Bourne, "Panic Disorder," *Help for Anxiety,* 2015, <http://www.helpforanxiety.com/panic_disorder.html> (February 10, 2015).

8. Donald J. Dalessio and Robert L. Goldstein, "Group Helps You Fight Fear, Depression," *San Diego Tribune,* February 20, 1990.

9. Anxiety Disorders Association of America, *Consumers' Guide to Treatment*, Anxiety Disorders Association of America, Rockville, Md., 1991, p. 3

10. Arthur Decker, personal interview, St. Louis Park, Minn., April 26, 1994.

11. Ibid.

12. National Institutes of Mental Health, "Anxiety Disorders: Diagnosis and Treatment," *National Institutes of Mental Health*, n.d., <http://www.nimh.nih.gov/health/topics/anxiety-disorders/index.shtml#part6> (February 10, 2015).

13. Ibid.

14. Morton S. Silverman, "It Sounded Exciting to Me," *P.M. News: Special 20th Anniversary Issue* (White Plains, N.Y.: Phobia Clinic of White Plains Hospital Center, September/October 1991), p. 7.

15. Ibid.

16. Ibid.

# Glossary

**agoraphobia** —The avoidance of a particular place or situation because of the fear of having a panic attack there.

**alcoholism**—A disease in which a person has an overwhelming desire to drink alcoholic beverages.

**anxiety**—A feeling of unease and distress that may not be related to any particular object or situation.

**behavior therapy**—This treatment helps people change and gain control over their unwanted behaviors.

**censorship**—The practice of preventing the publication or distribution of materials that people in authority object to.

**cognitive therapy**—This treatment helps people change their self-defeating or distorted thoughts.

**coping**—Dealing with.

**hypochondria**—A condition in which someone is convinced that he or she is ill or is about to become ill and often feels real pain when there is no physical illness present or likely.

**irrationally**—Feeling something that is not based on facts or reason.

**MAOIs**—Monoamine oxidase inhibitors, drugs that helps people decrease their anxiety.

**panic attacks**—A sudden, unexplained period when a person reacts to an extreme fear, although there is no cause for fear.

**phobias**—An irrational, intense fear of an object or situation.

**predisposition**—Tending toward something based on having inherited it.

113

**psychiatrist**—A physician specializing in disorders of the mind.

**psychologists**—People who specialize in the study of the mind and behavior.

**social phobia**—An intense fear of situations in which the person could be watched and judged by others.

**specific phobia**—An unreasonable, persistent fear of an object or situation. The most common specific phobia is fear of animals.

**superstition**—The belief that an object, action, or circumstance will influence the outcome of an unrelated event.

**theories**—Ideas that explain facts, observations, or events.

**therapist**—Someone trained to provide treatment for illnesses, disabilities, or other conditions.

**therapy**—Treatment to help someone overcome an illness, disability, or other condition such as a phobia.

# For More Information

**American Psychiatric Association**

1000 Wilson Boulevard

Suite 1825

Arlington, VA 22209

(888) 35-77924

psychiatry.org/

**American Self-Help Group Clearinghouse**

(973) 989-1122

http://search.selfhelpgroups.org/selfhelp/

**Anxiety and Depression Association of America (ADAA)**

8701 Georgia Avenue

Suite 412

Silver Spring, MD 20910

(240) 485-1001

adaa.org/

**Life Skills Education**

314 Washington Street

Northfield, MN 55057

(507) 645-2994

lifeskillsed.com/

**Mental Health America**

2000 N. Beauregard Street

6th Floor

Alexandria, VA 22311

(703) 684-7722

mentalhealthamerica.net/

**National Institutes of Mental Health (NIMH)**
6001 Executive Boulevard
Rockville, MD 20852
(301) 443-8431
nimh.nih.gov/

**National Alliance on Mental Illness (NAMI)**
3803 N. Fairfax Drive
Suite 100
Arlington, VA 22203
(800) 950-6264
nami.org/

**The National Panic & Anxiety Disorder News (NPAD News)**
npadnews.com/

## TREATMENT

**Agoraphobics Building Independent Lives (ABIL)**
3212 Cutshaw Avenue
Suite 315
Richmond, VA23230
(866) 400-6428
anxiety-support.org/

**Agoraphobics in Motion (A.I.M.)**
P.O. Box 725363
Berkley, MI 48072
(248) 547-0400
aimforrecovery.com/

**The Anxiety & Phobia Treatment Center**
41 East Post Road
White Plains, NY 10601
(914) 681-1038
phobia-anxiety.org/

**Freedom From Fear (FFF)**
308 Seaview Avenue
Staten Island, NY 10305
(718) 351-1717 ext. 20
freedomfromfear.org/

**Midwest Center**
12300 Wilshire Boulevard
Suite 325
Los Angeles, CA 90025
(866) 771-9858
midwestcenter.com/

**Phobics Anonymous World Service Headquarters**
P.O. Box 1180
Palm Springs, CA 92263
(760) 322-2673

**Recovery International**
105 W. Adams Street
Suite 2940
Chicago, IL 60603
(312) 337-5661
recoveryinternational.org/

**TERRAP**
755 Park Avenue
Suite 140
Huntington, NY 11743
(631) 549-8867
anxietyandpanic.com/index.php

# Further Reading

## Books

Garber, Stephen, Marianne Garber, and Robyn Spizman. *Monsters Under the Bed and Other Childhood Fears.* New York: Villard Books, 2011.

Matthew, Hal. *Un-Agoraphobic: Overcome Anxiety, Panic Attacks, and Agoraphobia for Good: A Step-by-Step Plan.* Newburyport, Mass.: Conari Press, 2014.

Milosevic, Irena, and Randi E. McCabe (eds.). *Phobias: The Psychology of Irrational Fear.* Santa Barbara, Calif.: Greenwood Publishing Group, 2015.

Pittman, Catherine M. *Rewire Your Anxious Brain: How to Use the Neuroscience of Fear to End Anxiety, Panic, and Worry.* Oakland, Calif.: New Harbinger Publications, 2015.

Stossel, Scott. *My Age of Anxiety: Fear, Hope, Dread, and the Search for Peace of Mind.* New York: Random House, 2014.

U. S. Department of Health and Human Services, National Institutes of Health, and National Institute of Mental Health. *Anxiety Disorders.* North Charleston, S.C.: CreateSpace, 2013.

Van Ingen, Daniel J. *Anxiety Disorders Made Simple: Treatment Approaches to Overcome Fear and Build Resiliency.* Eau Claire, Wis.: PESI Publishing & Media, 2014.

## Video Resources

WebMD. "Too Scared: Social Anxiety Disorder." <http://www.webmd.com/anxiety-panic/video/too-scared-social-anxiety-disorder> (February 5, 2015).

PBS. "Understanding PTSD." <http://www.pbs.org/thisemotionallife/video/understanding-ptsd> (February 5, 2015).

# Web Sites

**mentalhealthamerica.net/conditions/phobias**

*Mental Health America provides information on the three main groups of phobias and how to treat them.*

**ptsd.va.gov/**

*The National Center for PTSD features the latest research and education on posttraumatic stress disorder.*

**socialanxietysupport.com/**

*Social Anxiety Support has a therapist finder, support group finder, and treatment reviews.*

**kidshealth.org/teen/your_mind/mental_health/phobias.html#**

*TeensHealth explains what fears people have and how fear works as well as what causes phobias and how to overcome them.*

# Index

## A

Acquired Immune Deficiency Syndrome (AIDS), 30, 66
acrophobia (fear of heights), 48, 67
aerophobia (fear of flying), 34, 49
agoraphobia, 13, 21, 26, 27–28, 33, 34, 35, 42, 51, 76, 78, 79, 83, 93, 98, 101
Agoraphobics Building Independent Lives (ABIL), 93
Agoraphobics in Motion (AIM), 93
agrizoophobia (fear of wild animals), 73
ailurophobia (fear of cats), 34, 51, 52
Albano, Anne Marie, 19
alcohol, 15, 28, 33, 42, 90–91
amaxophobia (fear of driving), 52
American Psychiatric Association, 13, 19, 24, 100
antidepressant, 8, 98
Anxiety and Depression Association of America (ADAA), 85, 91–92, 94, 97, 100
Anxiety and Phobia Treatment Center, 101
apiphobia (fear of bees), 47, 52, 54
aquaphobia (fear of water), 49–50
arachnophobia (fear of spiders), 54
astraphobia (fear of lightning), 56

## B

bactrachopobia (fear of reptiles), 56
Beatles, The, 64
Bonaparte, Napoleon, 34
botanophobia (fear of plants), 56
Bourne, Edmund, 89
brontophobia (fear of thunder), 56
Bunyan, John, 40
Burton, Robert, 40

## C

caffeine, 78, 89, 90

carcinophobia (fear of cancer), 22

claustrophobia (fear of enclosed spaces), 13, 34, 52, 57, 67

cryophobia (fear of cold), 57, 59

cyberphobia (fear of computers), 59, 72

cynophobia (fear of dogs), 59, 81

**D**

Decker, Arthur, 97

demophobia, *See* ochlophobia.

dental phobia (fear of dentists), 15, 59

depression, 15, 28, 33

*Diagnostic and Statistical Manual of Mental Disorders* (*DSM*), 43

Doctor, Dr. Ronald, 51

dopamine, 78

**E**

enochlophobia, *See* ochlophobia.

entomophobia (fear of insects), 60

eremophobia (fear of being alone), 60

exercise, 89

**F**

fear

  becoming a phobia, 13, 19, 21

  irrational, 10, 33

  rational, 10

fight or flight reaction, 12, 95

Franklin, Aretha, 34

Frederick the Great, 34

Freedom From Fear (FFF), 51, 101

Freud, Sigmund, 34, 43

**G**

Garber, Dr. Stephen, 22

gephyrophobia (fear of bridges), 48, 60

gerascophobia (fear of getting old), 60

Gookin, Dan, 72

**H**

Hardy, Dr. Arthur B., 101

hemophobia (fear of blood), 22, 60

Henley, Arthur, 79

Herskowitz, Dr. Julian M., 78

Hippocrates, 40

Hitler, Adolf, 63

Houdini, Harry, 34

Hughes, Howard, 35

hypochondria, 30, 65

hysophobia, *See* acrophobia.

**J**
Johnson, Samuel, 42

**K**
King, Larry L., 81

**L**
lachanophobia (fear of vegetables), 63
Le Camus, A., 40
Levinson, Dr. Harold, 78

**M**
meditation, 88
melophobia, *See* musicophobia.
Mental Health America (MHA), 92, 100
microphobia (fear of germs), 35, 63
Midwest Center for Stress and Anxiety, 101
murophobia, *See* musophobia.
musicophobia, 63–64
musophobia, 65, 73, 81
mysophobia, *See* microphobia.

**N**
National Institute of Mental Health (NIMH) 43, 45, 92, 100
neophobia, *See* tropophobia.
nosemaphobia (fear of illness), 65

nosophobia, *See* nosemaphobia.
numerophobia (fear of numbers), 66
nyctophobia (fear of night), 66

**O**
occupational phobias, 67
ochlophobia (fear of crowds), 67, 73
ochophobia, *See* amaxophobia.
odynophobia (fear of pain), 22
ombrophobia (fear of rain), 68
ophidiophobia (fear of snakes), 68, 73
ornithophobia (fear of birds), 68

**P**
panic attack, 8, 26, 27, 51, 78, 88, 95, 98, 100
panphobia (fear of everything), 35
papyrophobia (fear of paper), 68
phobia
   definitions, 10, 19, 21, 42
   related problems, 33
   statistics, 14, 28, 33, 51, 72, 79, 85
   types of, 17, 21
   universal, 83

*phobos,* 39
Poe, Edgar Allan, 34
positive imagery, 88–89
public speaking
    fear of, 17, 18, 24, 70
    treatment of, 70
pyrophobia (fear of fire), 67

**R**
Recovery International, 94
relaxation, 88, 95
reptiles, fear of, 18, 56
Rolling Stones, 64
Rush, Benjamin, 42, 60

**S**
scoleciphobia, *See*
  vermiphobia.
scolionphobia (fear of school),
  70
Scott, Willard, 34
serotonin, 98
shyness, 24, 25, 34
Simon, Carly, 34
social phobias, 21, 22, 24–25,
  26, 28, 31, 34, 70, 76, 79, 83,
  101
specific phobias, 21, 28, 79, 83
superstitions, 30

**T**
technophobia (fear of
  technology), 72

TERRAP (TERRitorial
  APprehension), 101
tobacco, 90, 91
topophobia (stage fright), 34
traumatophobia (fear of
  injury), 60
triskaidekaphobia (fear of
  thirteen), 66, 72
tropophobia (fear of making
  changes), 73

**V**
vermiphobia (fear of worms),
  73

**W**
Watson, J. B., 81
Westphal, Otto, 42

**X**
xenophobia (fear of strangers),
  73

**Z**
zoophobia (fear of animals),
  73